What people are saying about …

Fun Loving You

"Ted Cunningham's *Fun Loving You* is a brilliant, original, and fresh work that delivers on its promise to take your marriage to a new level!"

Gary Thomas, author of *Sacred Marriage* and *The Sacred Search*

"Norma and I enjoy spending quality time with Ted and Amy Cunningham. They know how to enjoy life and each other. I laugh out loud every time we are together. This book is a fun, practical, and witty read. If your marriage is stuck in a rut, *Fun Loving You* is the jump start you've been looking for."

Dr. Gary Smalley, bestselling author and speaker

"Those who know Ted Cunningham from a distance recognize him as an innovative pastor and gifted teacher, but those of us who know Ted well know he's a party on wheels. I can't think of a better person to help infuse our marriages with more love and laughter. Who doesn't need joy like this?"

Margaret Feinberg, author of *Wonderstruck*

"*Fun Loving You* is a book that makes you laugh while challenging you to love well and act better in your marriage. It's smart and practical and gave me new ideas on how to chase the girl of my dreams—even after thirty-nine years of chasing."

Ed Gungor, lead pastor of the Sanctuary in Tulsa, OK, and *New York Times* bestselling author

"Ted Cunningham did it again! *Fun Loving You* is witty, entertaining, and profound. It will unstick even the most stuck marriage. Ted's authenticity will encourage you, make you smile, and give you hope. This book will get your priorities back on track to love, serve, and spend time with your spouse!"

Ryan Carboneau, American Association of Christian Counselors in Forest, VA

"If I could listen to only one guy speak about marriage for the rest of my life, it would be Ted Cunningham! No one blends humor, Scripture, and a passion for healthy, vibrant marriages like he does. Ted has spoken at North Point Community Church a couple of times at our MarriedLife Events, and his content never disappoints. *Fun Loving You* is the perfect combination of practical teaching, real-life experience, and a lot of laughter."

Jána Guynn, multicampus MarriedLife director at North Point Ministries, Inc., in Alpharetta, GA

"Two of the most endearing qualities about Ted Cunningham radiate through this book: his nonthreatening approach and practical wisdom. You will laugh out loud as you read and will be inspired to seek the same feelings you had with your spouse when you first began dating. With humor and examples from his own marriage, as well as exercises, tools, and suggestions for the reader, this is the most practical marriage book I've ever read. If you're tired of the rut, *Fun Loving You* is sure to get you out of it."

Dr. Joshua Straub, The Connextion Group

"Ted Cunningham has a passion to help couples develop and maintain loving and honoring marriages. In his book *Fun Loving You*, I believe he has developed tools that will help you find the kind of deep satisfaction from your marriage that he and his precious wife, Amy, have found in theirs. This book is full of questions, fill in the blanks, conversation starters, and date ideas for couples. I recommend this for engaged couples, newlyweds, or couples who have found themselves just not having fun anymore!"

Joe White, author, speaker, and
president of Kanakuk Kamps

"Ted Cunningham writes books that are truly helpful for couples who want to grow together. *Fun Loving You* flows from the heart of a couple who deeply love Jesus and each other. Ted and Amy are a living testimony to the advice given in these pages. I highly recommend you read and enjoy this book together as a couple."

Mark Connelly, lead pastor of Mission
Community Church in Gilbert, AZ

"Ted Cunningham gets it. Starting with his very first paragraph, he shows you how to have a vibrant, fun-filled marriage. And what

I love the most is that he and his wife, Amy, live in the real world and know how to relate to our lives."

Dan Seaborn, speaker, author, and
founder of Winning at Home

"My good friend Ted Cunningham is perhaps the most gifted communicator and author on the subject of marriage and family in America today. His new book, *Fun Loving You*, is another reason I feel this way. Marriages are under attack like never before. Work on your marriage! This book will help you do that."

Dr. Alex Himaya, founding and senior
pastor theChurch.at in Tulsa, OK

"As usual, Ted cuts to the chase and gets right at the heart of what tends to cause couples to drift toward dysfunction, resentment, and sometimes divorce. I especially appreciate that Ted gives so many practical ideas, including the 'list' suggestion, to help us keep our marriages healthy and vibrant and fun!"

Debbie Chavez, director of the wives'
ministry Squadron of Sisters and faith-based
talk-show host at www.faithplace.org

"A good marriage takes a ton of intentionality. *Fun Loving You* gives us fun, practical tools to make even the most stuck-in-the-grind marriage better."

Eric and Jennifer Garcia, cofounders
of Association of Marriage and Family
Ministries in Scottsdale, AZ

"Whether as a communicator or author, Ted has a uncanny way of breathing fresh life into your marriage and relationships. I'm confident this book will not only replenish your marriage, but spark new memories as well!"

Adam Donyes, founder of Kanakuk
Linkyear in Branson, MO

"If you are wanting to add a dose of fun to your marriage, *Fun Loving You* is the right medicine! Practical and insightful, this is a book you won't want to put down. Ted does a great job describing the energy that comes to the marriage by adding fun to the relationship. It is a must-read no matter what the phase of your marriage."

Rich Shanks, marriage ministry director at
Southeast Christian Church in Louisville, KY

"The church in this post-Christian era is fully engaged in a war for the preservation of marriage. Ted Cunningham has proven once again to be an experienced, trusted, and valued ally of the church in this fight! This book is a *must-read* for every couple who truly seeks to improve the quality of their marriage."

Jim Bolen, care ministry pastor at Savannah
Christian Church in Savannah, GA

"Ted Cunningham inspires me to be a strategic husband. The principals in *Fun Loving You* will ensure that my wife and I are best friends regardless of our circumstances. Simple. Funny. Insightful."

Shay Robbins, men's director at
Kanakuk K-2 Kamp in Branson, MO

fun loving you

enjoying your marriage in the **midst** of the grind

ted cunningham

David C Cook®

transforming lives together

FUN LOVING YOU
Published by David C Cook
4050 Lee Vance View
Colorado Springs, CO 80918 U.S.A.

David C Cook Distribution Canada
55 Woodslee Avenue, Paris, Ontario, Canada N3L 3E5

David C Cook U.K., Kingsway Communications
Eastbourne, East Sussex BN23 6NT, England

LCCN 2013943295
ISBN 978-1-4347-0456-6
eISBN 978-1-4347-0717-8

© 2013 Ted Cunningham

The Team: Alex Field, Nicci Hubert, Nick Lee, Caitlyn Carlson, Karen Athen
Cover Design: Amy Konyndyk
Cover Photo: Veer Images

Printed in the United States of America
First Edition 2013

3 4 5 6 7 8 9 10 11

120914

*I dedicate this book in honor of Lloyd and
Lorraine Freitag's sixty-five years of marriage.
Amy and I praise their love.*

Contents

Acknowledgments

Thank you to my friends at David C Cook. Alex Field, here's to another book. This is our sixth project together, and I am grateful for your friendship and encouragement. Thank you to Don Pape, Terry Behimer, Ingrid Beck, Annette Brickbealer, Ginia Hairston, Caitlyn Carlson, Renada Arens, Nicci Jordan Hubert, Jack Campbell, and the rest of the editorial, sales, and marketing teams for their faithfulness, passion, and expertise. Thank you, Lisa Beech, for tirelessly scheduling (and rescheduling) radio and television interviews for this book.

God has blessed me with many tremendous friends and mentors in ministry. Gary and Norma Smalley, Joe and Debbie Jo White, Jim and Judy Sedlacek, Doug and Dee Goodwin, Travis and Kari Brawner, Doug and Sonya Hayter, Mike and Tann Gattis, Greg and Erin Smalley, and Bill and Carolyn Rogers are key leaders in my life.

Woodland Hills Family Church supports my passion for marriage and family. They send me out each weekend to challenge and encourage couples and parents. Thank you to the elders, staff, and congregation for your hard work in Branson and around the world. Denise Bevins, you are the best. I am grateful for your patience in managing the details of my life. Thank you, Stephanie Watson, Joshua Straub, Felicia Pettigrew, Corinne Simmons, Tiffany Powers, Jennelle Pettigrew, Katrina Cramer, Ryan and Brenda Pannell, and Matt Gumm for your contributions to this book.

I am also grateful for Mission Community Church in Gilbert, Arizona. Thank you, Mark and Kay Connelly, for your friendship and partnership. I love the team at Mission. Thank you, Kevin Rhineheimer, Gary Sutliff, Matt Engel, Spencer Brannan, Ed Gungor, David Gungor, Lisa Devereaux, Will Sutliff, Randy Thomas, Rick Prigge, Jessica Pohle, Abby Andrus, Lissette Lent, and Paul Yerrick. A fun group to serve alongside.

Finally, I am grateful for the love and support of my wife. She takes part in every book. She and our children allow their lives to be on display. I do not take that for granted. I love you, Amy, Corynn, and Carson.

Introduction

Thanks for joining me on this journey in *Fun Loving You*! As the founding pastor of Woodland Hills Family Church in Branson, Missouri, and author of several books on marriage and parenting, I have a passion to help people develop and maintain loving and honoring marriages … which is easier said than done. If you've opened this book, you've likely come to the table with a marriage that you know can be, well, more *fun*. It's so easy to get caught up in the seriousness of life. But in *Fun Loving You*, it is my goal to help you learn (or relearn) how to *enjoy* life with your spouse and family amid the daily grind.

Amy and I have been married for seventeen years, and we have a marriage mission statement that reads, "We choose to honor, enjoy, and prioritize our marriage until either one of us lays the other in the arms of Jesus or the Lord returns." We live each day with this mission in mind. We choose every morning to esteem each other as highly valuable, to eradicate the kid-centered home, and to make each other laugh. It hasn't always been easy, but it has been deeply fulfilling, and over the years, I've developed tools that I know will help you find the kind of deep satisfaction from your marriage that Amy and I have found in ours.

This book is full of hundreds of questions, fill-in-the-blanks, conversation starters, and date ideas for couples. At the end of each chapter, I give you time to interact in your own Fun Loving You journal. Your journaling will include questions to ask your spouse and yourself, as well as plenty of ideas to help you start dating and planning quality couple time out of town. Use what works best for you and your spouse.

I would love to keep up with you. As you and your spouse discover new ways of enjoying life together, please send out a tweet with #funlovingyou. I will be watching and stealing your ideas for my marriage.

Blessings,
Ted Cunningham

Chapter 1

Love, Laughter, and a Trampoline

*A cheerful heart is good medicine, but a
crushed spirit dries up the bones.*
—Proverbs 17:22

One of my primary missions in life is to make Amy Cunningham laugh. Sitcoms have laugh tracks. Comedians have happy drinkers on the front row. Preschoolers have Tickle Me Elmo. I need none of that.

One way in which I accomplish this mission is by modeling my wardrobe choice for her each morning. After dressing, I step out of the closet and put my hands on the corner of the vanity. Then I drop my head like one of those New York runway models, lean my back end toward Amy, and say, "You want to tap it?" Trust me, it is not a sexual move. She breaks into laughter every time.

When was the last time you and your spouse laughed out of control? Amy and I got on a roll a few months back while jumping on our family trampoline. Yeah, I know what you're thinking, *Shocker, a family in the Ozarks with a trampoline.* We keep it next to the inflatable pool and my truck. When I assembled the trampoline, I thought it would be for the kids. I was wrong. I had no idea how much fun a married couple could have on one of these Walmart specials. When I say fun, I mean in the daylight and at night.

It's hard to be mature on a trampoline. There's nothing like coming home exhausted from a long day at work and being asked by your seven-year-old, "Hey, Dad, you want to jump on the trampoline?" Your first answer is probably the same as mine. We know the right "let your kids know you love them" answer. However, my heartfelt answer is, "That's the last thing on earth I want to do right now."

Nevertheless, we take off our shoes, unzip the safety net, and roll onto the fifteen-foot-in-diameter mesh. After three or four jumps the static electricity builds up and our hair stands on end. When you see an adult jumping on a trampoline, you never think, *Well, look at that; there's a responsible adult.*

Not taking yourself so seriously is the first step toward bringing laughter into your marriage. Being a responsible adult does not mean that you must remain serious at all times. Self-deprecating humor goes a long way in building intimacy in your marriage.

God wants you to laugh.

We need to laugh in the midst of the grind. The grind may be one reason why the average child laughs some four hundred times per day compared to the average adult laughing only fifteen times a day. If we let it, the grind can rob us of our sense of humor.

Solomon shares with us that laughter is an important season of life and a break from the grind. Laughter is given to us as a time of refreshment, just like the seasons: "There is a time for everything, and a season for every activity under the heavens" (Eccles. 3:1). God has appointed the seasons of our lives. They are part of His creation. There is "a time to weep and a time to laugh, a time to mourn and a time to dance" (v. 4).

The Maker of heaven and earth set our planet on an axis of 23.5 degrees. That's what gives us our seasons. The Creator did this for us, and He says in verses 2 through 3 that there is an appointed time to be born. There is an appointed time to die. There is an appointed time to plant and an appointed time to uproot. There is an appointed time to kill, an appointed time to heal, an appointed time to tear down, and an appointed time to build.

He has even given us an appointed time to laugh (v. 4). The almighty Creator of heaven and earth gave us laughter as a season. In extreme climates, there are only two seasons, a rainy season and a dry season. What season is your marriage in right now? Is it in one of those dry seasons where everything is a fight? If I can be blunt, some of you are currently in a "too serious" season. Laughing to you seems childish and immature. Lighten up. Your spouse will thank you, and you will live longer.

I think somewhere along the line Christianity has taught that marriage and adulthood are about long faces and being serious all the time. I can always tell when I walk into a church whether laughter is permitted. You see it on the faces. Thank you, Woodland Hills Family Church, for your ability to laugh. We take God seriously, but not ourselves.

How else is laughter good for you? Proverbs 17:22 says, "A cheerful heart is good medicine, but a crushed spirit dries up the bones." Could you use a little dose of this medicine? Drs. Les and Leslie Parrott find that laughter has benefits for your health:

> The healing power of laughter was not taken seriously by a scientific world until the late Norman Cousins, former editor of *Saturday Review* and subsequently professor at UCLA's School of Medicine, wrote about his life-changing experience with humor. As he reported in his book *Anatomy of an Illness*, laughter helped turn the tide of a serious collagen disease. "I made the joyous discovery," Cousins reported, "that ten minutes of genuine belly laughter had an anesthetic effect and would give me at least two hours of pain-free sleep." He surrounded himself with Marx Brothers films and *Candid Camera* videos. He also checked out of the hospital and moved into a hotel, where, as he says, he could laugh twice as hard at a third of the price.
>
> Cousins called laughter "inner jogging" because every system in our bodies gets a workout when we have a hearty laugh. Laboratory studies support Cousins's hunches. Our cardiovascular and respiratory systems, for example, benefit more from twenty seconds of robust laughter than from three minutes of exercise on a rowing machine. Through laughter, muscles release tension, and neurochemicals are released into the bloodstream, creating the same feelings long-distance joggers experience as "runner's high." [1]

I think it is time to make room in our lives for some YouTube clips. Your home needs laughter to reduce stress, improve health, and create a bond with your spouse and children.

Try it right now. Just tighten up your stomach and start laughing. You can even fake laughing if you don't feel like genuinely laughing. Have you ever noticed that spontaneous laughter is contagious for your family? Somebody starts laughing and then you start laughing. You walk into a room where people are laughing, and it immediately brings a smile to your face. That is the power of laughter.

Preacher Henry Ward Beecher said, "A person without a sense of humor is like a wagon without springs. It is jolted by every pebble in the road. Good humor makes all things tolerable."

Airports are at times intolerable, and for that reason I love making Amy laugh at the security check-in. She knows I love the screening where you stand in the 360-degree X-ray scanner. If they are going to see me naked, I'm going to give them a show. When invited to stand on the two yellow feet, I plant myself and launch into a one-man dance party. Amy loves hearing the TSA agent say, "Sir, we need you to stand perfectly still." No problem.

The best way to avoid a pat-down at the airport is to act like you want one. When the TSA agents size you up for the "special treatment," give them a gentle nod and inviting wink. It throws them off every time. They immediately wave you through. I have had 100 percent success with this method.

"Laugh out loud," said Chuck Swindoll. "That helps flush out the nervous system."[2] On another occasion Chuck said, "Laughter is the most beautiful and beneficial therapy God ever granted humanity."[3]

Milton Berle said laughter is an "instant vacation."

Jay Leno said, "You can't stay mad at somebody who makes you laugh."

Bill Cosby said, "If you can find humor in anything—even poverty—you can survive it."

Essayist and biographer Agnes Repplier, who was known for her common sense and good judgment, said, "We cannot really love anybody with whom we never laugh." I agree. [4]

I met Amy in April 1995. We were students at Liberty University, and a mutual friend set us up on a blind date. It was a clear night on Smith Mountain Lake, where we sat across the table from each other on a dinner cruise. She was (and still is) smoking hot. I was as nervous as a pig at a Hormel meatpacking plant. I wish I could say we laughed our way through dinner, but we barely spoke. It was awkward for me because I literally was speechless in her presence. Even though I struggled through dinner, it was all the time I needed to decide she was the one.

When the cruise returned to the dock, I told our buddy of my intentions to marry Amy. He laughed.

"Ted Cunningham!" he said with a look of shock. He could not believe that I could make a decision that quickly.

"I'm serious, Austin; I want to marry her. She is the one." I spoke with calm and resolve. The picture of our marriage and family was clear in my head.

I knew I had to do something to blow her out of the water and clearly state my intentions. Since I was the coordinator of the cruise, I took a couple dozen of the flashy Mylar balloons from the boat back to school with me that night. I wrote a letter to Amy sharing with her my excitement from the evening. I then asked her roommate to place the balloons and note in her room.

When Amy returned after chapel, the mass of balloons caught her off guard. She read the letter and thought, *Was Ted on the same date I was?* She considered our first date a dud.

She spent that summer on a mission trip, and I sent her a few letters to keep in contact. They were short and to the point. My plan was to lie low through the summer, then reignite the sparks upon our return to Liberty in the fall.

It took the entire semester for our young love to bud. There were several moments while dating where things were shaky. Nothing unusual, just typical relationship-formation bumps in the road.

But by Christmas, we knew marriage was close. I asked her to marry me in May 1996. We married on October 19, 1996.

Seventeen years of marriage, two kids, a mortgage, and a minivan later, I am crazy in love with Amy Cunningham. Not a day goes by that we don't laugh, dream, play, and enjoy life together. Every day we make the decision to lighten up and pursue a fun marriage.

If you followed us around for a day, you would probably say, "These two are boring." Our day-to-day routine is similar to most couples. We raise kids, make meals, work jobs, pay bills, clean house, attend church, take out the trash, do the dishes, help with homework, change lightbulbs, plunge toilets, get ready for bedtime, and wake up the next day and do it all again. Our daily grind is predictable, and I love it.

Our life and marriage are not drawing the attention of any Hollywood screenwriters. It would take quite a bit of embellishment to make it a blockbuster movie. (However, if I had to pick two actors to play Ted and Amy, I would choose Vince Vaughn and Reese Witherspoon. We relate to them the best on the big screen.)

The first seven years of our marriage were like most marriages. We shifted our attention from similarities to differences. We realigned our expectations with reality. We fought over money. We felt misunderstood and at times devalued. We went to bed angry and quiet on many nights.

Our marriage was in the grind, yet we knew there had to be a better way. We felt stuck, and we wanted to be unstuck. We knew the grind was here to stay, so we figured we should try doing something else. We didn't want to medicate our way through the grind, and we had no plans to look for someone else. The grind was unpredictable, and we had no control over it. So we decided to change our approach rather than find an escape.

We remembered all the fun times we had while dating in college and wondered if returning to those days was even possible. We wanted the romance, passion, desire, and sparks. Many senior couples we talked to would tell us, "Welcome to the real world." "You can't have those feelings and good times forever." I refused to accept that.

So we asked ourselves, "What is the formula for a fun, loving marriage? What will it take to enjoy life again? Enjoy marriage? Enjoy each other in the midst of the grind?"

If we stopped bringing up controversial discussions, would escalated arguments go away? If we downplayed differences and focused on similarities, would the sparks return? If we quit our jobs and moved somewhere different, would a change of scenery bring back the excitement? What if our marriage is missing children? Would we be happier if we made more money?

A fun, loving marriage is not found in the answers to any of those questions!

To begin enjoying life and marriage in the midst of the grind, we needed a paradigm shift in our thinking. Enjoying marriage and each other is possible in the midst of controversial issues, differences, pain, hard work, toddlers, and a tight budget.

The formula for a fun, loving marriage is not all that complicated and is found in three simple words: *honor, enjoy,* and *prioritize.*

Honor

First, when you're stuck in the grind, you must esteem marriage and each other as highly valuable. Hebrews 13:4 states, "Marriage should be honored by all, and the *marriage bed kept pure, for God will judge the adulterer and all the sexually immoral.*" At first glance we tend to focus on the "*marriage bed kept pure*" section of Scripture. To do so overlooks the clear teaching that each of us must lift high the institution of marriage.

Every day Amy and I strive to paint a beautiful picture of marriage to our kids, family, and friends. Through our social media outlets we raise the flag of marriage and encourage people to invest in their marriages. We do not run each other down, make fun of each other, or criticize each other to family and friends. We believe that marriage should be safe and shouted from the rooftops.

Part of honoring marriage is honoring each other. Amy is personally autographed by God, and I want to show her that value each day. Some marriage ministries have a take on this message: "God gave you your spouse to beat you down and suck the life out of you so you can be more like Jesus." Is this really the picture of marriage we want to paint?

Honor decides. It makes a decision to esteem as valuable. God did not ordain marriage to be a miserable weight you wear your entire adult life to bring you closer to Him. A fun, loving marriage starts by raising the value of your marriage and spouse.

Enjoy

Second, in the midst of the grind you must enjoy life together. Ecclesiastes 9:7–9 says to "go, eat your food with gladness, and drink your wine with a joyful heart, for God has already approved what you do. Always be clothed in white, and always anoint your head with oil. *Enjoy life with your wife, whom you love, all the days of this meaningless life that God has given you under the sun—all your meaningless days.* For this is your lot in life and in your toilsome labor under the sun."

You and I have a responsibility in the daily grind. Dare I say part of your purpose in life is to play and have fun? Yes! You are called to enjoy life! This is a message we lost years ago.

When you're stuck in the grind of life, enjoy life. Live life! Pursue it! Decide to not waste it! Find those precious moments in sharing a meal, laughing, and being joyful. Life is difficult, yes, but you can decide to find those moments and enjoy each other. You can't escape the grind, and for goodness' sake, do not turn your spouse into the grinder.

God did not give me my spouse as part of the grind. Amy and I are going through the grind together. You do not have to choose between life and a spouse. You can enjoy life with your spouse in the midst of the grind.

Prioritize

Third, in the midst of the grind you must prioritize your marriage in the home. Amy and I tend toward a kid-centered home, but we fight against it every day. We know it's not good for us or for the kids.

Parents of generations past used to remind their children regularly, "The world does not revolve around you."

My daughter, Corynn, knows that she is my princess. She also knows that Amy Cunningham is the queen of our home. No one speaks when the queen is talking. No one runs ahead of the queen. When the queen picks a restaurant or activity, no amount of whining from the kids deters me. Our course is set.

My wife likes being the queen. The kids and I like her in the role of queen. But she rarely takes advantage of her esteemed position because she knows it destroys the lesson we are trying to teach Corynn and our son, Carson. Regularly I remind our kids, "I'm not perfect, but I am trying my hardest to show you both how a queen should be treated."

Corynn is convinced that our home has enough room for two queens. The fact is, there is room for only one.

Our children have a front-row seat to our marriage. Two great gifts we can give our children are a mom and a dad who enjoy life together and the hope of a great marriage of their own. Prioritizing marriage in the home paints a beautiful picture of marriage, which can be done by either a married parent or a single parent. When parents misunderstand the parent-child bond, their marriage and children suffer. So give your children the gift of a great marriage.

Genesis 2:24 prioritizes marriage: "That is why a man leaves his father and mother and is united to his wife, and they become one flesh." The bond between husband and wife is glue-like and meant to be permanent this side of heaven. That is not the bond we have with our children. Amy and I grow in oneness by prioritizing our marriage in the home.

A fun, loving marriage may not be as hard as you think. I believe the decision to enjoy life together flows from the same place where you made the decision to get married and stay together. It comes from the same place where you decide that your children are valuable. Your character makes the decision to enjoy life together.

If you are a conservative Christian who has strong doctrine and a divorce-proof marriage, my prayer for you is that you move beyond just enough to stay together. Make the time and do the hard work to enjoy life together.

If your marriage is in crisis, my prayer for you is that you will find hope again. Jesus breathes life into dead people, and I believe He breathes life into dead marriages.

The FLY Journal (#funlovingyou)

Do we have a vacuum of intimacy in our home and marriage?

Do I take myself too seriously?

How can we better cut loose and enjoy one another?

If our family and friends described the levity of our marriage, what would they say?

If our siblings were here and told a funny story about us, what would they say?

Chapter 2

The Unstuck Marriage

Enjoy life with your wife, whom you love, all the days
of this meaningless life that God has given you under
the sun—all your meaningless days. For this is your lot
in life and in your toilsome labor under the sun.
—Ecclesiastes 9:9

I enjoy counseling stuck couples. The issues vary, but the roots are the same. In-laws, jobs, homes, communication, ministry, leadership in the home, laziness, nagging, holidays, and unresolved anger are all issues that couples share as the source of the problem. For some, money and the lack thereof causes them to seek an emotionally detached third party in a pastor. Some point to parenting styles and their inability to get on the same page with discipline strategies. A sexless bedroom also leads couples to schedule that first appointment.

Most counseling appointments follow a similar pattern. I invite the couple into my office where I have a love seat. (For years I had a couch, but it worked against me. The husband would sit on one end and the wife on the other. I replaced the couch with a love seat to help the couple connect.)

I start by asking the wife, "What brings you in today?"

The wife says something like, "I can't give anymore. I give and give and give, and he does nothing in return. I want to talk. He doesn't. I want to go somewhere special every now and then. He doesn't. I want our marriage to go somewhere. He doesn't. I'm done. I'm tired of being the only one who gives. I've got nothing left to give."

Then I ask the husband, "What do you see as the problem in your marriage?"

Generally men are uncomfortable with counseling. It has nothing to do with their marriage, but it has everything to do with an environment where we discuss feelings.

He says, "I thought we were fine. I didn't realize there was a problem. I'm really hearing this for the first time." Of course he thought they were fine. He enjoyed taking what she gave. Something must change.

Every couple, whether they are in counseling or not, experiences the grind. When a marriage gets stuck in the grind, the vacuum of intimacy sucks each spouse dry. It is exhausting and draining.

Amy and I spent the first years of our marriage stuck in the grind. For us, it would come to a head every three months. We didn't schedule it. We didn't make it happen. It just happened. The stuckness led to what we call the QMR—quarterly marriage realignment. Because I withdraw from conflict and hard conversations, issues went unresolved for months.

Pastor Bill Hybels from Willow Creek Community Church uses the term "the last 10 percent," because in conflict we generally share 90 percent of the problem with little blood, sweat, or tears, but the last 10 percent is the elephant in the room—the part that leaves the relationship at risk.

When the relationship is at risk, couples are stuck. Sadly many marriages end because one or both spouses blame issues and each other as the source of the problem. There is a way out of the stuckness. There is a way to enjoy life and marriage at the same time.

Amy and I love to study the Wisdom Literature of the Bible. Years ago, the Lord led us to study Ecclesiastes, and it changed our lives and marriage. How in the world could this dark and seemingly pessimistic book of the Bible encourage our marriage? Great question. I want to show you. To get unstuck as a couple, you must change your fundamental beliefs about the grind and your marriage's place in it.

In Ecclesiastes 1, Solomon uses word pictures from creation to explain life in the grind. There is a pattern to life and every single person on planet Earth experiences it:

> Generations come and generations go,
>> but the earth remains forever.
> The sun rises and the sun sets,
>> and hurries back to where it rises.
> The wind blows to the south
>> and turns to the north;
> round and round it goes,
>> ever returning on its course.

All streams flow into the sea,
>   yet the sea is never full.
To the place the streams come from,
>   there they return again. (Eccles. 1:4–7)

Here we get the picture of a grinder. The earth was here and churning long before my mother conceived me. Just like you, I was born into the grind. The churning never stopped. It is as sure as the sun rising and the sun setting. It is as sure as rivers flowing into the sea. The grind gives us plenty of hard times and challenges throughout life. But keep in mind, God already knows about the grind:

> To Adam he said, "Because you listened to your wife and ate fruit from the tree about which I commanded you, 'You must not eat from it,'

> "Cursed is the ground because of you;
>>   through painful toil you will eat food from it
>>   all the days of your life.
> It will produce thorns and thistles for you,
>>   and you will eat the plants of the field.
> By the sweat of your brow
>>   you will eat your food
> until you return to the ground,
>>   since from it you were taken;
> for dust you are
>>   and to dust you will return." (Gen. 3:17–19)

God gave Adam work to do before sin entered the picture. However, grinding work became part of the equation as a result of Adam's disobedience. "Just as sin entered the world through one man, and death through sin, and in this way death came to all people" (Rom. 5:12). The grind is the direct result of humanity's fall in the garden.

How long will the grind last? The days may feel like they pass slowly, but the years pass quickly. We are not here long. The Bible says that this life of trouble and sorrow will quickly pass:

> Our days may come to seventy years,
>   or eighty, if our strength endures;
> yet the best of them are but trouble and sorrow,
>   for they quickly pass, and we fly away. (Ps.
>   90:10)

Age will not get you out of the grind. Even if you make it to eighty years of age, your life will be tough. Trouble and sorrow in this text mean gruesome, difficult, and painful, and it's a myth to think that the more years you get under your belt the easier the grind will get. Money cannot buy your way out of it. Degrees cannot outsmart it. Age and maturity won't deliver you from pain and trials.

Eventually your body will find its way into the grind. I love to read Ecclesiastes 12 to Amy at night to help us both picture our senior years on the front porch, rocking away:

> Remember your Creator
>   in the days of your youth,

before the days of trouble come
    and the years approach when you will say,
    "I find no pleasure in them"—
before the sun and the light
    and the moon and the stars grow dark,
    and the clouds return after the rain;
when the keepers of the house tremble,
    and the strong men stoop,
when the grinders cease because they are few,
    and those looking through the windows grow
        dim;
when the doors to the street are closed
    and the sound of grinding fades;
when people rise up at the sound of birds,
    but all their songs grow faint;
when people are afraid of heights
    and of dangers in the streets;
when the almond tree blossoms
    and the grasshopper drags itself along
    and desire no longer is stirred.
Then people go to their eternal home
    and mourners go about the streets. (vv. 1–5)

You're in the grind all the way to the end, and your only way out of the grind is death. Are you encouraged yet? Life is hard, and then you die.

As I finished this manuscript, news broke of the retirement of Pope Benedict XVI. At the age of eighty-five, he decided to step down as the leader of the Roman Catholic Church. He said, "I am facing the final leg of the path of my life and I don't know what's ahead."[1] For the first time in six hundred years, the pope would resign because his body could not keep up with the demands of his office. The grind gets everyone.

We become fragile, and our bodies start breaking down. We lose our teeth. Our glasses get thicker and thicker as we lose our eyesight. We stay inside the house, and the sounds of the marketplace grow faint to us. We nap all day long and wake up every morning at 3:00 a.m. Walking becomes difficult for fear of stumbling. Our almond trees blossom, which means our hair is turning gray. At thirty-nine, I am already experiencing this. Then, right before death, sex becomes difficult if not impossible. The grasshopper starts dragging. Sexual desire is no longer stirred.

I love asking my wife this question: "Amy, will you still love me when my grasshopper's dragging?" And do you know what my wife says? I kid you not, she says, "I think I'll be all right." She then asks me, "What are you going to do, Ted, when your grasshopper starts dragging?" I say, "The Lord can take me home. Life will just be over." You laugh, but that's what the Bible says: "The grasshopper drags itself along and desire no longer is stirred. Then people go to their eternal home and mourners go about the streets." Once the desire for sex is gone, people are ready to go be with Jesus.

The bookends of Ecclesiastes tell us life is hard (chapter 1) and then we die (chapter 12). Here we go. Are you ready to turn the corner in this text? I am. In the midst of the grind God invites you to enjoy your life:

> Go, eat your food with gladness, and drink your wine
> with a joyful heart, for God has already approved
> what you do. Always be clothed in white, and always
> anoint your head with oil. (Eccles. 9:7–8)

You and I have a responsibility in the daily grind. Dare I say that part of your purpose in life is to play and have fun? Yes! You are called to enjoy life! In the midst of the grind that is life, while you're still alive, go and do something. Live life and enjoy it! You need to find and hold on to those moments—sharing a meal paired with pinot noir, laughing, roller-skating, hiking, and being joyful. Don't throw that out the window because life is difficult. We can do nothing to escape the grind. So in the meantime, choose joy. Choosing to enjoy life is a decision. Make that decision.

And for goodness' sake, stop treating your spouse as the grinder. She is not the grind. He is not the grind. The grind is the seventy to eighty years you have upon this earth, and God blessed you with a spouse to go through the grind with you. You have a grind companion. Just like my wife and kids coming along on a trip to be my travel companions and enduring all the airport stress, you and your spouse get to work through life's challenges together.

You can enjoy life with your spouse in the midst of the grind:

> Enjoy life with your wife, whom you love, all the
> days of this meaningless life that God has given you
> under the sun—all your meaningless days. For this
> is your lot in life and in your toilsome labor under
> the sun. (Eccles. 9:9)

This is the only place in the Bible where it says, "Enjoy life with your wife." You and I do not need to choose between the two, and one does not trump the other. You can have both because marriage enhances life.

I love hearing guys tell me, "I had all sorts of plans, dreams, and goals for the future, but then I got married" or, "My wife and I had all sorts of plans, dreams, and goals for the future, but then we had kids." Let me give you the Greek/Hebrew term for those statements: *hogwash!* Your spouse was not brought into your life to kill your fun, play, dreams, and goals. And your kids were not brought into your life to be a killjoy either.

The grind creates a vacuum of intimacy, laughter, and fun in marriage. To enjoy an unstuck marriage, you must make new decisions.

When I meet with stuck couples, I walk them through the following eight symptoms of a stuck marriage. Most couples drift into these symptoms. The trick is getting them to decide their way out. Let's look at these eight symptoms and the decisions necessary to enjoy an unstuck marriage.

1. When your marriage gets stuck in the grind, you blame your spouse as the source of the problem.

My wife is not my source of life. Neither are my kids, job, money, home, or possessions.

This is the first symptom of stuckness. I believe that every married couple experiences this symptom at some point. It usually occurs in the early years.

When you look to your spouse as the source of life, you blame him or her as the source of all your problems. And when your spouse is the source of your problems, you automatically become dependent on him or her to create a solution. You are stuck, waiting on your spouse to make the first move. When your breakthrough hinges on your spouse's move, you start saying things like, "If he would just do this." "If she would stop saying this, we would be well on our way." Blame ends almost immediately the moment you realize your spouse is not your source of life.

In 1 John 4:16 we read, "And so we know and rely on the love God has for us. God is love. Whoever lives in love lives in God, and God in them." How many times have we seen that verse yet we forget that no matter how hard we try, we cannot generate, produce, or manufacture love and forgiveness? It's impossible because we are not the source. We forgive because He first forgave us. We love because He first loved us. He is the only source.

According to best-selling author Dr. Gary Chapman, a love language is the way we give and receive love. My wife, Amy, has two love languages: acts of service and quality time, which means I serve her for long periods of time. (That is our little joke.)

Did you know that God has a love language? God has a way that He gives and receives love as our source of life. As a pastor I hear many people say, "I don't feel connected to God." "I don't feel like God hears my prayers." We know the verse "I am the way and the truth and the life. No one comes to the Father except through me" (John 14:6). Most of us use that verse in the context of evangelism, speaking of the exclusivity of Jesus. There is no other way to the Father, amen. It's not only the way we come to the Father, but it's also the way we stay connected to the Father, through Jesus. The gospel is not for unbelievers alone. The gospel is for Christians.

God is our source of life, and we connect to Him through a vibrant and passionate relationship with Jesus.

Here is how Jesus described God's love language in John 14:23–24: "Anyone who loves me will obey my teaching. My Father will love them, and we will come to them and make our home with them. Anyone who does not love me will not obey my teaching. These words you hear are not my own; they belong to the Father who sent me." We abide in Christ and His words. He is the giver of all life. He is the source. In Him we live and move and have our being (Acts 17). We were created by Him and for Him.

Let's do a quick little exercise. Before you plug into the True Source, you must unplug from your spouse. With passion and a deep breath, raise your right hand and repeat after me, "I, [state your name], do hereby resign as general manager of the universe of my spouse. I am officially before God unplugging from my spouse as the source of life." There, don't you feel better? Now, take your finger and point it at your spouse. If your spouse is not present, pretend. Again with passion say, "You're fired!" Take a few moments with your spouse and explain what you just did. You just fired your spouse as the source of life.

When your spouse is your source of life, you spend your days trying to control, manipulate, and change him or her into your image. That's exhausting. Take it from me, a control freak. It's exhausting pastoring, fathering, and husbanding when you run around policing everyone all day long. Unplugging gives you room to breathe.

I love teaching this principle of unplugging to my kids. Underneath our kitchen sink, I keep a clear plastic jug. It's called the "Love Jug." When I pull the jug out, my kids scream, "*No*, not the Love Jug!"

I place the Love Jug on the counter and surround it with glasses of all different shapes and sizes. The glass for Mom is curvy. *Va-va-va-voom!* Corynn and Carson have slightly smaller glasses. We have glasses for teachers and for our church family and staff.

From the hose on the sink I fill up the jug and ask, "Who is the source?"

The kids respond with, "God."

"That's right. And our job is to connect to Him and allow Him to fill us every day. Then we go out and give our family, friends, and strangers the overflow," I say. As I pour from the jug into the individual glasses, the jug empties. Then I ask, "How do I replenish the water that I poured out? Do I wait for others to pour back into me?"

"No, God refills you," my kids say. My heart skips a beat when I get a glimpse of my kids understanding codependence.

When we spend our lives waiting for others to pour back into us, we live in codependence. We live on empty, disconnected from the True Source.

Do you want to enjoy life with your wife? It starts by unplugging from her as the source of life. God gave me my spouse so she and I could walk through the grind together. She is my best friend. But Jesus is my source for sanctification, not Amy.

2. When your marriage gets stuck in the grind, you question your compatibility.

Have you seen those eHarmony and Match.com commercials? They are inspiring. There is usually a smiling couple twirling around on the screen, talking about how great marriage is for them. That part I love. We need more couples painting beautiful pictures of marriage. However, at first glance I believe their message is misunderstood. Great marriages are not the result of great chemistry and compatibility. Great marriages flow from great character.

People watching is one of my favorite hobbies. In particular, I spend my waiting time at airports identifying online couples. They are easy to spot. It starts with a hesitant yet relieved meeting at the bottom of the escalator on the other side of security. Millions of couples meet online every year. Where do most of them meet for the first time? Airports.

Last year, Amy and I took the eight-minute shuttle ride from the Denver International Airport to the car rental facility. I eavesdropped on the couple sitting across from us, and I knew immediately they were an online couple meeting face-to-face for the first time. He was eating popcorn from a plastic grocery bag. She clenched her purse as though someone was out to steal it. He had a relaxed posture. Her posture screamed, "Am I safe with this guy? Oh, I hope he doesn't kill me and chop me up into a bunch of little pieces."

I nudged my wife and said, "Hey, an eHarmony couple." She gave me a nod that said, "Be good."

I pulled my phone out of my pocket and acted as though I needed to text someone. I snapped a quick picture of the couple but had forgotten to turn off the flash. The guy jumped, looked at me, and asked, "Did you just take our picture?"

I categorized this as an inconsequential social arrangement, so I almost lied. Instead, I came clean. "Yes, sir, I did. I'm in town to teach a marriage conference, and I noticed you two. You guys met online, didn't you?"

"Yes," he said.

"I could tell," I responded.

After five minutes of free marriage advice, they asked me to take another picture of them. This time they posed for the shot.

The crux of my message to this couple was: "Character trumps chemistry and compatibility. Great marriages flow from character. A good match is a good start, but it will never sustain a thriving, intimate, and loving marriage. Only character does that."

My wife and I never took a test before marriage, but we know we are very different. Amy grew up in a denomination that taught her to be set free in Jesus. I grew up in an independent, fundamental, premillennial, King James Version–only Baptist church. Why is that a big deal? We process everything through our childhood and upbringing. I believe that if I disobey a speed limit sign God will be mad at me and I possibly could see jail time. My upbringing gave me a guilt-prone nature. My wife views all speed limit signs as suggestions for other people. Jesus freed her.

I grew up learning that savings was money you put away for a rainy day. She grew up learning that savings was the difference between the actual price and the sale price. We are on different financial spreadsheets.

When it comes to celebrating the holidays, she grew up at 1600 Pennsylvania Avenue. Okay, maybe not, but her decorations at Christmas rival the White House's. By the time I pull the fifty-seventh box of decorations down out of the attic each December, I am in no mood to celebrate the birth of my Lord and Savior.

The fun part of marriage is exploring and learning to enjoy those unique qualities in your spouse. Amy and I have a ball trying to learn new things about each other. We love telling stories about our childhood to gain deeper understanding and appreciation for each other's words and actions. In the next chapter, I will show you how to start your own Fun Loving You list. This list turns the negative, frustrating, and annoying into the positive, fun, and enjoyable. It will raise the value of your spouse, which in turn will increase your desire for him or her.

Your character, not your chemistry, determines your commitment to enjoy each other for life. Moral laxity is the number one cause of divorce in this country. Debt, adultery, and broken promises are symptoms of a spouse's lack of character. Shallow integrity leads couples to look for an easy out when they find themselves on the poorer side of "for richer or poorer" or on the sickness side of "in sickness and in health."

One trend I see in couples who hit the half-century mark and enjoy one another is that they have steadfast commitment. They weather storms together and come out on the other side stronger in their marital bond.

Please don't hear me saying "Chemistry is not important." It is. It's just not as important as character. Chemistry does not hold you to your vows, but character does.

Work on your character. Allow the Holy Spirit to call you by name on blind spots in your life and heart. Next time you see an online-dating commercial, don't be fooled. You are not stuck in your marriage because you didn't take a test before marrying. Your stuck state may have more to do with what is going on in your heart.

3. When your marriage gets stuck in the grind, you repeat mistakes and develop patterns.

Most stuck couples experience what Emerson Eggerichs calls "the Crazy Cycle." Insanity is defined as repeating the same thing over and over again and expecting different results. Proverbs refers to this when it speaks of the nasty habit of our household pets: "As a dog returns to its vomit, so fools repeat their folly" (26:11). Foolish people repeat mistakes. Wise people learn from their mistakes.

We all make mistakes. The real issue is whether we will learn from them. Couples will often say, "We've tried everything, but we cannot get any resolution to this issue. We don't know what else to do."

I argue that they have not tried everything. More than likely they have tried a few things multiple times. This pattern drains marriage of fun and intimacy. You begin to think, *We've been down this road before, and here we are again. Why can't we get anywhere with this? Why are we still fighting over the same old issues?*

These cycles are called scripts. Just like an actor picks up a movie script, memorizes and rehearses lines, then films the scene, couples do the same thing. Whenever an issue surfaces, they pull out the same old script and read it line for line. They repeat the same lines and make the same points. Exhausting!

Pastors and parents share this tendency. If you don't think the congregation or the child is understanding your point, simply repeat louder. Add passion. Get more emotional. Pound the pulpit or table. Pace back and forth. Seldom does that work.

Don't get louder and repeat; try something new. When your conversations feel stuck, approach them from a new angle. Amy and

I found a new communication skill that rocked our marriage. It's called LUV talk—listen, understand, validate.

Conversations flow so much better when you listen more than talk. You listen with your whole body. Remove distractions. Square off your body with your spouse's. Make eye contact. Focus on your spouse's words rather than formulating your next statement. And by all means, keep your mouth closed.

One little prop I love passing out in counseling and at conferences is a little Matchbox or Hot Wheels car. It represents drive-through listening. Remember the old days when your order was misunderstood at the drive-through?

You placed your order into that small silver box. "Yes, I would like a cheeseburger, fries, and a Coke."

The box talked back and said, "That's a chicken sandwich, onion rings, and a shake." How many times did the person inside taking your order get it wrong? You went back and forth through that box until the order was right.

That's why I love giving couples the little toy car. The spouse holding the car is the communicator. He or she is the only one allowed to talk. The spouse not holding the car is taking the order by active listening. Most couples scoff when I introduce this toy into their communication, but eventually they see it as a great prop for slowing down their communication and taking turns. It definitely falls under the "try something new" category.

The conversation progresses when you focus on understanding rather than being understood. The best way to understand is to repeat back what your spouse said, word for word, until you get it right. When you put his or her words into your body language and tone, it completely changes the meaning. Keep going back and forth until you see the emotional nuggets behind the words. Feel the words; don't just exchange them.

Watch what happens when you read the same words in different tones:

"Let's eat, Grandpa!"

"Let's eat Grandpa!"

See the difference a comma makes? The former statement speaks to enjoying a meal with your grandfather. The latter statement speaks to enjoying a meal of your grandfather. Big difference! Pass that toy car back and forth so you both have a chance to talk, listen, and feel understood.

Amy and I want validation of our thoughts and feelings as well as resolution to our issues. I don't need to explain away or fix anything. Validation in marriage is like the validation you get for your parking at a mall or restaurant. When the waiter or store clerk validates your ticket, it simply means you were there. That's all your spouse wants from you and your conversations. She wants to know, *My husband was here, heard me, and understands where I am coming from.* He wants to know, *My wife was here, heard me, and understands where I am coming from.*

Gary Smalley taught us LUV talk years ago. At times it feels unnatural and forced, but let me tell you, it keeps our conversations out of the grind.

4. When your marriage gets stuck in the grind, you rush decisions.

When a couple is stuck, they struggle to make wise and healthy decisions. No amount of education, experience, or money solves this problem. It is an emotional issue.

Speed and hurry are enemies of intimacy. When your marriage is stuck in the grind, you lean toward expedient rather than principled decisions.

Last summer on our way back home from Tulsa, Oklahoma, my family stopped for dinner in Joplin, Missouri. On the side road to Chick-fil-A, we passed an attorney's billboard that read, "Divorce: Fast and Easy."

In shock I told my kids, "That sign is only half-true. If your arm was hurting and I took you to the emergency room, one way to get rid of the pain would be to chop it off. It would be fast, but it would not be easy. You may be able to get a quickie divorce, but in no way, shape, or form will it be easy."

The weight of a decision determines the amount of time, thought, and prayer required. I believe Jesus breathes life into dead marriages. I believe in miracles. Sometimes they happen in an instant. Like a flash of lightning, the spouse wakes up and listens to the Holy Spirit calling him or her by name, and the marriage is saved. Other times the miracle is seen over the span of a few weeks, months, or years. Either way, healing the wounds of stuckness takes time.

I make bad decisions when I'm tired. Amy knows that major life decisions must wait until morning. When I am exhausted, I get snippy. A good night's sleep is a game changer. I am a morning person, so I have greater clarity around 6:00 a.m. My best decisions come when I am fresh and rested.

Stuck couples are anything but fresh and rested. When they walk into my office, I can tell just by the way they sit down. It's usually a plop on the love seat with a deep sigh. The sigh tells me, "Well, here we are. I don't see this doing much good. But, hey, we'll give it a shot." Stuck couples are exhausted. When their tanks get low, or empty, they lose hope.

The hopelessness caused by exhaustion is easy to spot. You know when a couple is at their limits. When their load exceeds their limit, they throw their hands up in the air and quit. Please hear this from the heart of a pastor who loves you: Never make a decision to walk away from your marriage when your load is exceeding your limit. Instead, get your tank refilled.

When your physical, emotional, relational, mental, and spiritual tanks are empty, that is a horrible time to make major decisions about your marriage. You are not thinking clearly.

When my car runs out of gas, I don't think, *Well, I guess I'll send it to the junkyard.* No way! I stop at my nearest gas station and fill up. As my son would say sarcastically, "Obviously!"

5. When your marriage gets stuck in the grind, you close your heart.

I must ask you a very important question: Is your heart open or closed?

The answer to that question determines everything about your life and marriage. A closed heart is numb, detached, distant, and angry. An open heart feels safe, nonthreatened, and willing to share.

A few years ago at a marriage conference, I met a woman with a closed heart. I spotted her closed posture from across the room. As she made her way over to speak with me, I braced for a tough interaction.

With a quivering lower lip and shaking head, she said, "Do you want to know why my husband left me?" She was mad. At first, I prayed. I did not immediately engage her.

Before I could get my first word out, she snapped and said, "He left me because he could not handle my success." She was steaming mad. This was the strongest, angriest woman I had ever met. Hands down.

"Ma'am, I don't know you, but can I have your permission to pastor you for the next five minutes?" I asked. She stood there silent for a moment, but then she conceded.

I continued, "You have the potential of being a very beautiful woman. I am speaking of the inner beauty of a gentle and quiet spirit taught in 1 Peter 3. Here's the problem. You have a ginormous chip on your shoulder. I do not know how it got there. I don't know how long it has been there. This I do know. You are 100 percent responsible for the chip."

She looked as though she was going to bolt. This is one of the few times in ministry when I braced for an uppercut. So I said, "I still have four and a half minutes.

"A wise man years ago taught me two great lessons about my heart. First, unresolved anger is like drinking poison expecting the other person to get sick. Friend, you are drinking this poison by the gallons. It is only hurting you, not the other person. Second, you never bury anger dead. You always bury it alive. My fear for you is that you will pass this anger on to or take it out on your son" (who was standing right beside her).

I finished by saying, "You must resolve your anger. Your success did not cause your divorce. The issue is rarely the issue. The only way to resolve your anger is to receive forgiveness from the True Source of life and then give it freely to every person who has ever hurt you."

The Holy Spirit called this precious woman by name. I looked past her anger and saw a little girl who was hurt. I love watching the Lord work in the hearts of people.

Anger has three primary sources: hurt, fear, and frustration. Anger is a secondary emotion. It's not a primary emotion. You always feel something before you get angry. Those feelings are amplified when your heart is closed.

Proverbs 4:23 says, "Above all else, guard your heart, for everything you do flows from it." Every word you say and every action you take flow from your heart. When you are stuck and your heart is closed, your marriage suffers. You have only one heart. It's the same heart that worships God, loves your spouse, and cares for your kids. To close your heart because of a past relationship means you close your heart toward your spouse. God designed you with one heart. Keep it open.

6. When your marriage gets stuck in the grind, you isolate yourself from others.

I always love when someone comes into my office and says, "Pastor, it is easy for you to talk about marriage so positively because you have a great marriage." That's one of the few times in the pastor's office that I want to bop someone right in the mouth. I say that in jest, but, boy, does that work me up. Great marriages don't just happen. Do you know why Amy and I have a great marriage? Because we married the right person? Because we took an online compatibility test? No! Great marriages are the result of hard work!

Let me give you a word picture I learned from Dr. Scott Stanley that I hope you never forget. Everybody falls in love with the front end of the puppy. You know where I'm going with this, don't you? We fall in love with the front end of the puppy, but every puppy has a back end. Every marriage has a back-end story. Every marriage has a story of struggle, pain, frustration, trials, and disagreements.

When you are stuck, you fall into arrogance and begin saying, "Nobody gets what I'm going through." "Pastor, you don't understand my struggles." "You can't relate to what I'm going through." That's just not true. You are duped into a lie Satan wants you to believe.

I love and support the National Institute of Marriage in Branson, Missouri. The Institute fights for marriages every week through an intensive marriage counseling program. About fourteen years ago Dr. Greg Smalley assembled a team of expert therapists to minister to couples. His goal was to become the Mayo Clinic for hurting and stuck couples.

The intensive marriage counseling program is for divorced, separated, or near-the-end couples. Each husband and wife needs to answer this question: Are you open to a miracle? If both spouses answer yes and they are not medicating with drugs or alcohol, then we invite them to Branson for a week.

The intensives consist of two therapists, five couples, four days, and eight hours each day. The couples sit in the same room on a U-shaped couch for all four days. God works miracles on that U-shaped couch.

On the first day of the intensives, couples share their marriage stories. When they return to their rooms that night, we want them to say, "Wow, at least we're not as jacked up as those other couples."

When you get stuck and isolate from others, you fall for the lie that no one understands what you're going through. That is not true. These couples have either divorced, filed the papers, separated, or they are considering divorce. Their stories may have different details, but the symptoms are the same.

When you feel stuck, press into biblical community. You need to hear "What you are going through is not unique to you. We've been where you are now. You can make it through this. We will help you."

7. When your marriage gets stuck in the grind, you doubt your future as a couple.

The church I grew up in hosted revivals twice a year. We invited an evangelist to our church outside of Chicago every spring and fall. I remember one time sitting there on Sunday night with seventy to a hundred people. He preached a hellfire-and-brimstone message for about forty minutes. Then we stood and sang "Just as I Am" for the invitation.

After the first verse, if no one came forward, he preached another minisermon and then we sang verse two. If no one came forward, we skipped the third verse entirely. To this day I have no idea why we skipped that verse. By this point, the evangelist showed considerable frustration. He told a tear-jerking story, then asked this question: "Do you know, that you know, that you know, if you died tonight, heaven would be your home?"

At ten years old, I vividly remember how infuriated I was by that question. I had accepted Jesus as my Savior two years earlier. My first thought was, *Well, I thought I knew, but when you put it like that, I don't know.* As I looked around the congregation, I thought, *I know everyone in here. We've all been saved multiple times. Mom, if I go forward, can we go home? I'll take one for the team.*

Am I against invitations or altar calls? Absolutely not! What am I against? I am against planting seeds of doubt. I loathe it.

Who is planting seeds of doubt in the soil of the decision you made on your wedding day? You stood before God and others to commit yourself to your spouse. You made a decision when you said,

> *I take you, _____, to be my husband/wife, to have and to hold from this day forward, for better or for worse, for richer, for poorer, in sickness and in health, to love and to cherish; from this day forward until death do us part.*

Use discernment around family and friends who plant seeds of doubt. They may be well-intentioned, but their comments build doubt and erode commitment. They sound helpful, but what they say is destructive:

"We want you to be happy." Unhappiness is a seed of doubt but not an excuse for divorce.

"You deserve better." Entitlement places your needs at the top of the list above your spouse.

"There's someone out there better for you." Incompatibility believes the grass is greener on the other side. Never forget, where the grass is greener there is a septic leak and it's nasty. Stay home and water your own lawn.

"No one should have to put up with that." Conflict is part of every marriage. Get beneath the conflict and focus on the heart.

"We have a _____ issue." Issues are rarely the issue. Emotions drive every issue in your marriage. Discover what the real issue is.

"You need some me time." *Independence* is a socially acceptable term for selfishness.

"I'd rather see a divorce than a murder." Minimizing excuses a "small" sin with a "big" sin. Both divorce and murder are bad and should be avoided.

"You've tried everything to make it work." Exhaustion is understandable but never an excuse for severing the marriage covenant.

"He/She has changed." Chemistry wanes. Changing personalities, jobs, opinions, and bodies are expected.

"He/She won't change." Believe in the power of the gospel. Jesus still breathes life into dead people (Eph. 2). The gospel does not make bad people good. It brings dead people to life.

Here are some practical ways to breathe life and hope into a dead or dying marriage. This goes for your marriage as well as a family member's or friend's:

- Get involved without taking sides. Fight as a team, not opponents. You are on the same team.
- Avoid blaming on issues and focus on the heart. Let your spouse know there is a heart issue, a bigger issue to deal with.
- Center the conversation on marriage, not divorce. Let your spouse know God's original plan for marriage, and divorce is not necessary.

8. When your marriage gets stuck in the grind, you explore other options.

I am sick and tired of fighting for a marriage only to find out that one of the spouses is already dating someone new. Come on! How in the world are we going to save a marriage and protect the future of your children when you are so stinking selfish with a boyfriend or girlfriend waiting in the wings? Your children deserve better.

I'm not a stalker, but I do check out Facebook from time to time. It absolutely shocks me when I see the photos of the new boyfriend or girlfriend before the divorce is even final. It says to me, "I never really tried. I know we met with Ted and tried to get help, but it just didn't work." Hogwash! Bologna! You didn't try. You had your options lined up. Fight for your marriage. Be a man! Be a woman! Give your children a fighting chance.

Oh, how the Enemy just eats this up.

Last April, I ate breakfast with Dr. Scott Stanley, a professor and researcher at the University of Denver. He gave me a definition of *commitment* that I absolutely love: "Commitment is making a choice to give up all other choices." That is the opposite of what we are brought up to believe. We are taught to keep our options open. This is why some marriage counselors drive me insane. They sit down with a couple, hear their marriage story, and assess, "I don't think there is any hope. This marriage is over." Jesus breathes life into dead marriages! There is hope no matter how stuck you are.

Do I believe there are valid reasons to divorce? Absolutely. Abandonment and persistent, unrepentant adultery to name two. However, we must always start with hope, not divorce. You may end up there, but we do not start there.

Where are you with these symptoms of stuckness? Maybe the first two or three? Maybe all eight?

Please don't give up. I promise you that enjoying your marriage in the midst of the grind is possible. The National Institute of Marriage has an 87 percent success rate with stuck couples. And get this: they do not define success as the couple just staying together. Their definition of success is a couple staying together and reporting higher levels of marital satisfaction.

That means these stuck couples headed for divorce now experience a joy in marriage that they never dreamed was possible. It is possible for your marriage too!

The FLY Journal (#funlovingyou)

Do I often blame my spouse for his or her moods, words, or actions?

In what ways are we incompatible?

Does my character need work? How so?

What are two or three issues where I find myself repeating mistakes and developing patterns?

Is our marriage drained of energy and intimacy?

Are we expedient or principled when it comes to making major life decisions?

If our hearts are closed, whom do we need to forgive in order to begin resolving our anger?

How do we eliminate threats to our marriage? Have we each made the choice to give up all other choices?

Chapter 3

The Fun Loving You Lists

We will praise your love more than wine.

—Song of Songs 1:4

I love duets. Remember the classic 1965 hit by Sonny and Cher? It does not matter what style of music you prefer, you can probably deliver a line or two of "I Got You Babe." If you close your eyes, it is easy to picture Cher flicking her hair back over her shoulders as she looks down on Sonny.

I'm a child of the eighties. Most of my favorite duets are from the mid- to late eighties. I was thirteen years old when Aretha Franklin and George Michael hit the charts with "I Knew You Were Waiting (For Me)." That same year a movie came out that debuted the Bill Medley and Jennifer Warnes hit "(I've Had) The Time of My Life." *Dirty Dancing* was not on the approved movie list at our church.

My roots are in country music, and I live in Branson, Missouri, so the best duet of all time goes to Kenny Rogers and Dolly Parton.

"Islands in the Stream" is still number 9 on Billboard's list of all-time best duets.[1]

But above all those great love songs, the Song of Songs is the ultimate duet. It's the greatest duet of all time, hands down. Verse 1 of the book declares the song as *"Solomon's Song of Songs."* When we see Song of Songs, it reminds us of the banner King of Kings and Lord of Lords. Solomon wrote over a thousand songs (1 Kings 4:32), and the eight chapters of Song of Songs are his greatest hits. These chapters come together to form the song above every song.

There are three main characters in this book. First, there is Solomon. We know a lot about him: he's the son of David; he is a shepherd-king with great wisdom and vast fortunes; he is a hard worker and a lover of horses (1 Kings 4:26).

We don't have the name of the second character, but we know she is a simple country girl. She is the Shulammite woman. The third group of characters is the daughters of Jerusalem. These are what I call the backup singers. They are the doo-wops. Every now and then, as this song progresses, they praise the love of Solomon and the Shulammite. They cheer on and validate the young budding love of this romantic duet.

We can interpret the Song of Songs in a couple of different ways. First, we can read it as an allegory. In other words, this book is painting a picture of God's intense love for you and me, and everything we read is a parallel between God and His children. Some commentaries use this interpretation method, but this approach is nonhistorical.

The second approach is literal. Even though the book uses word pictures, it is speaking directly to the romantic love between a husband and a wife. This is the preferred and historical approach to interpreting this book of the Bible.

Song of Songs is a love song between a husband and a wife. The poetic beauty of this song describes a fun, freeing, sexual, married love between a man and a woman.

Desire and Attraction Must Be Guarded While Dating and Prioritized When Married

Desire and attraction are like breathing when you are first dating. They require no conscious thought or hard work. Words like sparks and tingles describe the intensity of feelings you experience when you first meet and attraction sets in. It is a beautiful thing.

I validate these intense feelings in young people. I must. Why? Because these are the same feelings I want to encourage in married couples. To deny them in the early stages of romance builds only animosity and distance in the hearts of married couples.

By the way, being attracted to someone is not the same as lust. Parents and church leaders jump to cautioning young people on lust, when what they experience is a genuine, heartfelt attraction to the opposite sex. I believe experiencing that feeling is possible without undressing the other person in your mind. Noticing the beauty of another and saying, "Good job, God," is perfectly healthy.

Attraction and desire are like movie, music, and clothing preferences. Everyone has different tastes. We are attracted to different body types, hair colors, dress styles, complexions, and facial features.

Desire says, "I want you." Exclusivity says, "I want only you." The Song of Songs starts off with strong desire. The desire of this woman says, "I want you." However, all eight chapters of this book of the Bible build from desire and toward exclusivity.

The Shulammite woman initiates desire: ***"Let him kiss me with the kisses of his mouth—for your love is more delightful than wine"*** (1:2). She compares her love, desire, and attraction to wine—relaxing, intoxicating, full-bodied, warm, and rejuvenating. She pictures their future love as better than wine.

In verse 3 she speaks of his character: ***"Pleasing is the fragrance of your perfumes; your name is like perfume poured out. No wonder the young women love you!"*** She is attracted to his character. When his name is spoken, the women sigh.

We market products with desire. But rarely will you see a commercial on television linking desire and character. Desire is linked to sex, beer, attraction, parties, fragrances, and compatibility. You hear the message "I want to be with you." You won't hear "I want to be with your character."

The Shulammite woman wants to be with Solomon's character. Her desire to be with him physically comes after her desire to be with his character. In verse 4 she says, ***"Take me away with you—let us hurry! Let the king bring me into his chambers."*** Here is something we all relate to, especially early in our relationships. Desire is always in a hurry. Delaying desire is not easy. But, again, please hear this from the heart of a pastor who loves you: validate and express your desire in an appropriate context.

The Song of Songs backup singers validate this desire: ***"We rejoice and delight in you; we will praise your love more than*** *wine."* It is very important to note that family and friends have a role to play in validating love. When you see it, say it. For example, "I can't help but notice how you light up when she walks into the room." "I've never seen you like that around anyone else."

Are you a good backup singer? I love doo-wopping over love when I see it. I regularly walk up to strangers' tables at restaurants and praise the love that I see. My wife is usually to the car before she realizes that I stopped at a table to cheer on a couple enjoying each other.

On a recent trip to Gilbert, Arizona, my family and I ate lunch at a quaint little diner called Liberty Market. Across the room I couldn't help but notice a couple in matching Tough Mudder T-shirts. The Tough Mudder is an insane, high-adventure race that includes scaling walls, plodding through ice water, crawling through immersed pipes, and dodging electrified cables shocking you toward the finish line. Needless to say, I have yet to try this race.

This middle-aged married couple first caught my eye when the husband wrapped his leg with an Ace bandage before his lunch was served. Their laughter was contagious. They talked nonstop. I couldn't hear exactly what they were saying, but I assumed the conversation went something like, "What were we thinking! That was crazy!" This lunch was their race debrief. I am sure they walked through each segment of the race, recounting the obstacles to their mighty finish. They did not strike me as a couple concerned about placing; merely finishing sufficed. It was a ball watching them.

As I walked by their table, I had to sing them a line or two.

"Excuse me for interrupting, but I just wanted to say how much we enjoyed watching you two over lunch," I said. At first they looked at me as though I was on some sort of watch list.

"You two are very much in love?" I asked. Their defenses came down a bit as they looked at each other and smiled.

I continued with, "So, how was the Tough Mudder?"

They immediately started laughing at each other, and he said, "Crazy, but we had a blast."

I concluded by saying, "For the sake of your marriage, I hope you do it again next year." Then I turned and headed toward the car.

Backing up the duet of strangers may not be the best place to start, so try it out closer to home first. Give it a shot at your next family holiday. Over dinner, point out a couple and share all the great qualities you observe in their marriage. It is contagious. Watch how others follow suit.

Parents, are you backing up the young, budding love of your single children? Or does your concern for their independence, college degree, and success trump the prospects of walking down the aisle? When we see the heart experience love, let's not make the Christian mistake of automatically labeling it "lust." When you see desire and attraction build in your child, start with validation. Don't jump into a lengthy and boring discourse on purity. Validate the feelings first; then teach them how to guard their desires prior to marriage. Starting with the purity talk is like singing out of tune. Validation echoes the feelings of the smitten.

Be careful of your backup singers who are single or who are married but desire to be single. If you have friends who are prolonged adolescents, they may not be the best at backing you up. Marriage brings you into a responsibility and selflessness they know nothing about. So they won't know how to back you up. It may mean finding new friends or associating with different people, which is okay—your time is limited anyway. Jaded divorced people tend to make horrible backup singers. Limit your time with them if they constantly berate your marriage and sing out of tune.

I know this may sound harsh, but it is superimportant. As a pastor, I see a lot of jaded single parents who are lousy at backing up the love and marriage of their children. Such parents make two mistakes. First, they assume that their child's marriage will go down the same path as their own. Second, the jaded single parent can be selfish and struggle with relinquishing time with his or her child. A mom or dad with unresolved anger, bitterness, or resentment toward his or her ex can write negative and often false beliefs about marriage onto a child's heart. Do not allow a bitter parent to be your backup singer.

While I am going down Tough Love Street, I'll throw one more at you. Grumpy old people are also horrible backup singers. Please note, I did not say, "Old people." I said, "Grumpy old people." The key word there is *grumpy*. I have several senior men and women in my life who are pure joys to be around. They love Jesus and those around them, and they respond well to the trials of life. Yet, I know plenty of seniors who allow the pain and struggles of life to affect their attitudes in a negative way rather than a biblical way as outlined in James 1:2–4 and Romans 5:3–5. Never listen to the advice of one who says something bitter or negative like, "You'll settle down," or, "We were in love like that once; you'll get over it." Do not allow the negativity other people allow into their lives to become a part of yours. Enjoy life and marriage. Find loving, kind older friends, and model your marriage after theirs.

I believe the Lord called me years ago to teach the church how to be great backup singers for marriage. Many pastors called to the work of marriage and family ministry walk away from vocational pastoring to pursue parachurch ministry. Trust me, there have been many Monday mornings where that tempted me. However, I remain committed to cheering on and honoring marriage in the local church. I beg you, make sure that you serve in a local church that teaches the Bible with strength. Also, be part of a church that will back up your marriage. Biblical community holds Amy and me accountable. We choose to let them in and inspect our love for each other.

Whether one is single or married, insecurity becomes a barrier to attraction and desire. In Song of Songs 1:5, we see that insecurity is a roadblock to desire and attraction. When insecurity finds its way into a marriage and into the bedroom, exclusivity is threatened. The Shulammite woman says, ***"Dark am I, yet lovely, daughters of Jerusalem, dark like the tents of Kedar, like the tent curtains of Solomon."*** She has a tan. In that day, a tanned woman meant she worked outside and neglected her body and complexion. Today, tans are in. But in that day, paleness was beauty.

She continues down the road of insecurity in verse 6: ***"Do not stare at me because I am dark, because I am darkened by the sun. My mother's sons were angry with me and made me take care of the vineyards; my own vineyard I had to neglect."*** She speaks here of how her own body has not been taken care of because of a family issue. Her stepbrothers treated her poorly and forced her to work outside. Her insecurities mirror what many women struggle with today. Her two primary insecurities are with her family and her physical appearance.

Generally speaking, men and women have different insecurities. Have you ever watched what happens in a room when someone breaks out a camera? It's striking to me. The camera comes out and all the women start hiding. Just like movies where aliens are trying to figure out humans, women look at cameras as though it is a brand-new invention. "What is that, a camera?" "What are you going to do with that?" They immediately go into defensive mode, fearing Facebook and Twitter posts.

We have a dinner show in Branson called *Dixie Stampede*. It is set back in the Civil War. Before you enter the stadium, each family gathers for one large group picture. The picture is simply a memory of the time you spent with your family. It is candid, not studio quality. About thirty minutes into the show, a sweet young woman walks to each table and offers your group a photo package. My wife hates every picture. It's always a fun time for us before we even see the picture. As the woman hands it to us, I say to Amy, "We both know you ain't gonna like it."

How do men act when a camera comes out? It's a race to who can get the dumbest act recorded. We push each other out of the way to get to the front. We flex. We make faces. We hold a pose with pride.

The same is true of mirrors. Ever go to a gym? Women walk by mirrors. Men stop and stare. Just like the camera scene, we suck in our gut and give a flex as if to say, "Man, I am one good-looking dude."

Ladies, as a pastor, may I speak into your beauty for a moment? Stop comparing yourself to the supermodels. You do not employ full-time makeup artists. You can't afford professional trainers and nutritionists. When you walk by the magazines on the endcap, remember the Hebrew term for those covers: Photoshop. Those images have been heavily altered.

Guys, may I speak into your lives as well? You need to set the standard for beauty in your home. Set the standard of beauty to your wife and to your daughters. Don't miss this with your sons; explain to them what beauty is. There are many different body types. There are so many different looks. When the dad sets the beauty standard in the home, no comparison is necessary. May our kids regularly hear us complimenting the beauty of their moms.

This brings us to a point where we need to be confronted a bit. I need this as much as anyone. *Make an effort to be attractive for your spouse.* Before you attack me for being shallow, give this some time to settle in.

I am grateful Amy likes taking care of herself. She has many different looks, and I enjoy all of them. She has a sporty look that includes an athletic outfit, hair pulled back through a ball cap, and running shoes. She enjoys a casual jeans and T-shirt ensemble with a fleece. She has a vacation look that requires a pedi and mani before we leave. She has a formal party look that is stunning. I love them all.

I am the one who gets stuck with one look and feel. Jeans, shirt, dress casual shoes, and a North Face fleece scream comfort for me. When I walk out of the bedroom each day, I look the same. I bathe every day, brush my teeth, and get a haircut every few weeks, but left on my own I would wear the same three outfits for the rest of my life. I need to make more of an effort for my wife.

Some of you guys need to throw away the Old Spice and try some new cologne. You say, "Yeah, but I've been using Old Spice for thirty years." I know you like it, and I know your mom buys it for you every Christmas. Maybe it is time to mix it up a little bit and try something new. Let your wife pick.

I love standing in our closet and shouting out to Amy, "Hey, come in here and pick out which one of these outfits you would want to rip off of me later." She usually chooses the one with snaps, not buttons. *Bom-bom-chicky-chicky-bom-bom.*

Couples stop making an effort when their looks go unnoticed. This is a cycle we must break by offering regular, sincere compliments to our spouses. It can be something as simple as this:

"Honey, you are really looking good today," he compliments.

"No, I don't. My hair is giving me fits," she replies.

He tries again by saying, "Seriously, you look beautiful today."

She shuts it down with, "Yeah, you're supposed to say that."

Did you hear that? It is one thing to give a compliment, but of equal importance is the receiving of a compliment. Rejected compliments eventually lead to no compliments. The beauty is in the effort and the compliments.

Husband, start complimenting. Offer your wife more descriptive compliments about her beauty when you two are alone. Be open and frank. Declare before the kids, "Your mom is smokin' hot!"

Desire creates a longing to spend time together. The Shulammite woman says in Song of Songs 1:7, *"Tell me, you whom I love, where you graze your flock and where you rest your sheep at midday."* She wants a lunch date. She wants time in his schedule. Exclusivity prioritizes time together and makes less time for others. But in this request, she asks a very important question: *"Why should I be like a veiled woman beside the flocks of your friends?"* (v. 7). She is speaking of a prostitute. She says, "I'm not going to be that type of lunch date." Remember, they are dating and not yet married. She declares her desire but won't bend her character to win the man.

Solomon rolls up his sleeves and gets to work on her insecurity. This is the first time he speaks in the book. He uses a word picture rooted in his love for horses. I would not encourage you ever to compare your wife to a horse, but it works for Solomon: ***"I liken you, my darling, to a mare among Pharaoh's chariot horses. Your cheeks are beautiful with earrings, your neck with strings of jewels. We will make you earrings of gold, studded with silver"*** (vv. 9–11).

A mare is a female horse. As a collector of horses, he knows how all the studs respond when a mare walks by. According to 1 Kings 10:26, "Solomon accumulated chariots and horses; he had fourteen hundred chariots and twelve thousand horses, which he kept in the chariot cities and also with him in Jerusalem." He is pointing her out above all other women. Chariots in battle used black stallions. A mare harnessed to a chariot was rare. Again, his praise builds exclusivity.

Amy and I decided years ago to regularly remind ourselves and our kids of one another's value. I keep a running list of all the great and valuable qualities I see in Amy. She keeps one on me, too.

Our FLY (Fun Loving You) Lists

Gary Smalley is a marriage and family rock star. After forty-five years of ministry, Gary and Norma Smalley continue to minister to couples and families around the globe. Married for fifty years, they know what it means to have fun together. Gary often jokes, "I have made my living messing up in marriage, writing about it; then you people read it."

One practice that keeps Gary and Norma's love growing is the regular application of honoring each other. Honor esteems another as highly valuable. It is treating someone as a treasured gift that is priceless. Gary taught me years ago how to honor my wife every day and make her a priority. When I choose to honor Amy, the feelings of love, romance, and intimacy well up inside of me and affect my actions and attitudes. My desire for honor in our marriage is simple. Every day I want to think and say, "I am in the presence of someone really great."

When was the last time you turned to your spouse, with your jaw wide open, and said, "Amazing! Unbelievable! I can't believe it! I can't believe I am actually sitting next you"? The next time you walk into a room and see your spouse, fall on the ground and proclaim, "I'm not worthy! I'm not worthy!" You might hear "Get up, weirdo." Don't stop. Keep pursuing random acts of honor. You might feel a little uncomfortable at first—that's to be expected. But when you make such comments (and I encourage you to!), what you're really saying is that you can't believe that you are in the presence of someone very valuable—you are honoring that person. You're saying, "You're valuable to me! You're significant! You're worthwhile! You matter!"

Gary also taught me how to keep an honor list. He has lists in journals and on his computer that detail all the reasons why Norma Smalley is valuable. He has multiple versions of honor lists floating around his house and office. The last list I saw was over four pages long on a yellow legal pad.

I asked him, "Gary, how important are these lists?"

"They are key to keeping honor high in our marriage. Reading through these lists keeps me sane, in love, and having fun. Whenever Norma and I are in a disagreement, I go to the honor list. It only takes reading a few lines for me to remind myself why I love that woman," Gary responded.

His eyes get misty when he talks about the list. This is the most inspiring practice I keep with me.

My mom turned sixty-four years old this year. I've known her for thirty-nine years, and there is no gift left to buy her. When I was little, I purchased just about every cheap bottle of perfume Osco Drug displayed. One year, my brother and I had our portraits taken together, and that lapse in judgment still hangs on her wall. She needs no more dishes, cat calendars, sweaters, knickknacks, clocks, wall art, doilies, or candy or cookie tins. All she wants is family.

I think from here on out, special dinners out with no price limit will do. Mom, order from the left side of the menu, not the right. In other words, order what you want with no thought on prices.

For Mom's sixty-fourth birthday, we took her to the Sunday brunch at the Chateau on the Lake here in Branson, Missouri. The dining room was full, the food was spread, and a senior adult played tunes on a piano. Perfect atmosphere for celebrating the life of a loved one.

About halfway through the meal I asked each member of our family to share something extraspecial about Pama (that's what her grandkids call her). The request alone brought tears to her eyes. As we worked our way around the table, here is what we shared:

1. She always thinks of the needs of others, not hers.
2. She forgets nothing! She has a file in her brain
   on every family member and friend. When you

share something with her, post on Facebook, etc., she never forgets it. Then when she shops, she looks for what she can buy that person based on his or her desires, not hers. She buys nothing for herself. She sees it as a waste of money. For example, she labors for years before buying a new phone or computer.

3. Bottom line: most giving person I know.

4. She is our family historian. She is taking over this role from my grandma, Mary Jane Ludwig. Her strongest desire is to keep her family connected. I lost count on how many times she calls my brother, hands me the phone, and says, "Here, talk to your brother."

5. She loves small children and is a grandma to many. I am blown away by her capacity for relationships. Her social calendar exhausts me. I can't keep up.

See now why twenty-five-dollar gift cards are fleeting? When we speak words of blessing over someone, it is like a huge gust of wind blowing into a sail. Our parents want to know they did a good job. Your time with family may be limited, so make the most of it.

Probably the most natural and easiest blessing is the one we give our kids. I have heard some pretty spectacular blessing stories over the years, but my favorite is that of Roger and Michael Gibson.

Roger is Michael's dad. They both are passionate golfers and spend countless hours each year on the links. Roger understands how important it is to speak encouraging words over one's children, and no one does it better. He inspires me.

For Michael's sixteenth birthday, Roger worked out a special surprise birthday blessing. He invited his son to the golf course for a round. But this day would be different. Instead of two bags and one cart, only one bag was necessary. Roger caddied the first hole for his son. He used that time to speak blessing and picture a special future over his son.

When they reached the second hole, Roger's caddying was over. Mom waited to caddy that hole for her son. I picture them walking down the par 4, talking about life and the sixteen years of Michael's life. I have no idea what was said, and I don't want to know. That was a moment for mom and son.

Grandpa caddied the third hole. I know he cried, because it was Grandpa Gary Smalley. My love and respect for Gary lead me to believe he invented the blessing and honor. He loves his grandson deeply. Investing words of high honor into Michael is something he continues to this day.

There is no need to list all the family and friends who caddied for Michael that day. Hole after hole, Michael heard words of honor. Words that esteemed him as highly valuable. Words that cherished who God created him to be.

Now here's the most important question: Do you think Michael has forgotten the words spoken to him on that day? No way! They burned into his brain, and like tattoos on the heart, they are there to stay. That is the power of spoken words of blessing.

Why is it so easy to do this with parents and children, and yet we labor to do this for our spouses? This is bothersome to me. Words of blessing and honor over Amy should flow off my tongue. I wonder why it is easier to keep lists in our brains of all the frustrating, nerve-racking, annoying pet peeves but such a struggle to find the words to say, "You are highly valuable!"

Mining for Gold

One of my family's favorite television shows is *Gold Rush*. This show was "like at first sight" for the Cunningham family. It shocks us how much grueling work goes into gold mining. The risk is huge. Thousands of dollars and work hours are spent with the hope of finding some flakes of gold in the bottom of a pan.

Every episode is similar in pace and story line. The process starts by staking a claim. The claim owners or tenants decide which piece of ground to mine. The land is rugged and thick in the Alaskan and Yukon wilderness. A bulldozer strips the ground and removes the top layers of mud. When they get close to bedrock, they hope for a pay streak. That means they are on the gold and getting it out of the ground is all that's left.

After the ground is stripped, next comes the excavator. The dirt is placed in a dump truck and hauled to the wash plant, where another excavator awaits. The pay dirt is stockpiled next to the plant, and the excavator feeds one bucket load at a time into the top of the wash plant, where water is mixed with the dirt. This begins the process of separating the dirt from the gold. The dirt, rock, and sand kicked out the back of the plant are what they call the tailings. The finer material travels through a sluice, where metal grates and mesh carpets trap the gold. Since gold is heavier than dirt, the finer and lighter material is washed out of the plant and the gold remains. But hold on—they are not done yet.

The grates are removed, and the carpet is carefully gathered and placed in the back of a John Deere Gator. The carpets are washed out in a large metal cow trough. The water is drained, and what looks like thick black sand remains. Now the panning begins. Each pan is gently manipulated in a counterclockwise pattern. After a few minutes, the gold appears. You see it in their eyes. Like kids' eyes on Christmas morning, their bright eyes tell the story. Unless of course there is no gold. Then their eyes turn sad, followed by a hand to the face and a "you've got to be kidding me" sigh.

During this entire mining process, the gold miners stop to fix broken machinery, drill holes to test new ground, place the skids back on the dozer, race against time as the snow thaws and creates a soupy mess, hold meetings with investors, work through personal conflicts, miss family and friends back home, and battle exhaustion and sleep deprivation. I'm sticking with the pastorate.

All of this hard work, sweat, fighting, bleeding, and stressing is done in the hopes of finding a few flakes of gold. Most episodes, no nuggets or flakes are found, just fine gold dust. Seriously, these men and women spend months and months processing thousands and thousands of yards of dirt in the hope of leaving the Klondike with a jar or two of gold.

I love watching seven to eight big guys who need a bath in a bad way stand around one guy's open palm to inspect a few tiny flakes of gold. Is it worth it? Yes!

This entire show is a metaphor for marriage. As I watch it on my DVR each week, I so wish couples would start mining each other. What is the payoff in marriage of a couple investing years of hard work, energy, money, time, breakdowns, injury, sickness, sleep deprivation, exhaustion, and miscommunication? I think the payoff is huge even if you see only dust at the beginning. There is value in your spouse; you just need to look for it.

How much time, blood, sweat, and tears are you willing to spend mining for a few nuggets?

Amy and I want to be great miners. We started major mining last year, and we developed a twist with our lists. We call ours the Fun Loving You lists. We don't have volumes or multiple versions lying around the home or office, yet, but we have a great start. The ground is stripped, and the pay dirt is stockpiled.

Every time a frustration, pet peeve, irritation, hang-up, disagreement, or difference of opinion surfaces, we add it to the list. We treasure hunt how to have fun with it. Treasure hunting is mining for the gold in every situation.

Here are our lists.

What I Love about Amy

1. I love your "all or nothing" passion. You do nothing halfway. When you start a project, you finish it with gusto. You inspire me to work hard and get it done.
2. I love your disdain for directions. You love letting me lead. You couldn't care less how we are getting there. While driving or at airports, you pay no attention to signs because you completely trust me to get you there.

3. I love your eye for design. You make our home and our church beautiful places to live, serve, and worship. I never get the vision at first, but once the space is complete, all I can say is, "Wow!"

4. I love your selfless serving. From sunrise to sunset you never stop serving your family. Your family and friends are always comfortable when you serve them.

5. I love your attention to detail. You leave no stone unturned when it comes to doing things right. From planning our vacations to making dinner reservations, you know at what time of day we will be hungry three months from now.

6. I love your lists that keep our family organized. They are more like gentle reminders than honey-do lists.

7. I love your adventurous culinary spirit. My favorite meal once was meat loaf, mashed potatoes, and corn. Not anymore. You have elevated my palate. Bring on the heat, spices, texture, and plating.

8. I love your confidence. You are secure in who you are as a wife and mom. This is one of your most attractive qualities.

9. I love the fact that you do not have a people-pleasing gene. You do not strive to meet the nonstop and at times excessive expectations that people place on you. I actually envy this about you.

10. I love that you prioritize our marriage. You have eradicated the kid-centered home and place

our marriage first. Date nights are important to you. You help me model a great marriage for our kids.

11. I love how you love Carson. Even though you need to stop calling him "pooh bear," you let him be all boy. When he comes into our room in the middle of the night, you are never frustrated to meet his requests.

12. I love how you love Corynn. You let our daughter be her own person in personality and all of her pursuits. As she begins individualizing as a young adult, you allow her to develop her own tastes of clothes. I know how hard that is for you, but you are so gracious with her.

13. I love how you take care of yourself. You are smokin' hot!

14. I love your "roll out the red carpet" hospitality. No one throws a dinner party like Amy Cunningham! You spend weeks planning and executing the perfect party.

15. I love your confidence in my expertise on everything. You ask me questions, believing I know the answers to everything from astrophysics to nuclear proliferation. It amazes me how much you think pastors know.

16. I love how you picture a very special future for our family. You have big dreams and plans for our family. Never stop dreaming, my love!

17. I love your commitment to Christ. You are sensitive to the Lord's leadership in your life. When I see you reading your Bible in the morning while sipping your coffee, that is when you look your sexiest. Thank you for placing your relationship with Christ before me. This is the true secret to a fun, loving marriage. I am not your source of life.

18. I love how you share everything. You are constantly thinking about who can use this more than us.

19. I love it when you say, "I don't want anything to eat; I'll just take a bite of yours." I am more than willing to buy you your own entrée or dessert, but I love that you want me to order.

20. I love how you let me find my own parking space. There is not a lot of adventure left for men in the world anymore, so you let me have this final frontier.

21. I love your multitasking. You can watch a movie, read a magazine, and surf Pinterest all at the same time. Amazing. What a gift!

22. I love your spontaneity. With two to three days' notice, you cut loose and go with the flow. My favorite line is when you tell me, "Just call me Flo."

23. I love your equilibrium. You know when the house feels 70.5 degrees. When you ask me, "Did you change the thermostat?" my answer is always

the same: "I haven't touched the thermostat for the past fifteen years." I love it when you kick off the bottom corner of the sheets to expose your left foot. Then I know you are the perfect temperature.

24. I love how you protect me from hot things. You are constantly jumping in between me and a hot curling iron.

Amy has a list for me.

What I Love about Ted

1. I love your implied questions that you deliver with strength. My favorite question is, "I look really good in this outfit, huh?"

2. I love your travel agent abilities. You get so excited about planning trips for our family. The fact that you know how many miles, points, down-to-the-minute times of arrivals and departures, layover times, which restaurants we have to choose from at the various concourses, etc. The fact that you keep this all in your head is amazing.

3. I love that you are always concerned about my comfort when it comes to temperature. You are constantly offering me your coat and even your socks when necessary. How many movie theaters have we been to where I am comfortable and you are freezing?

4. I love how the child in you comes out when you get to build a fire. You get such a feeling of accomplishment, and it is displayed in your body language and on your face once the fire has taken off.

5. I love your competitive nature that peaks when we play board games. You obsessively count your money in Monopoly as if it was the real deal.

6. I love your fiscal responsibility. The fact that you always know how much money I spent at Target before I ever get home. And when you greet me at the door to help me with my bags and quote how much I spent, you do it with a smile on your face that genuinely says, "I hope you had a good time."

7. I love your skillful exaggeration. I know the marriage experts say humor does not work in diffusing escalated conflict, but somehow you make it work.

8. I love how easy you are to please. Whether we have cereal for dinner or filet mignon, you say, "That was a perfect dinner!"

9. I love how you make me feel like the most important person in the room. You include me and our marriage in every conversation.

10. I love how you lead our family spiritually. You seize those teachable moments and are very intentional about leading us through God's Word.

11. I love how you see potential in me that I do not see in myself. You have a way of encouraging

me to stretch myself. You give me the blessing every day.

12. I love the way you dream. Without you, I would not take the time to dream. Whether it be a trip we may take someday or a project we would like to complete, I always have something to look forward to in our future.

13. I love how you do the dishes and make the bed every single day! It is automatic for you.

14. I love how you lead us in prayer as a family every single night. We pray with gratefulness for what God allows us to do as a family. Our kids are catching the vision of the ministry that the Lord gave us.

15. I love how you always drive even when you are really tired. You know how much I hate driving and navigating. I am there for conversation when you need me.

16. I love your dependability. You do what you say you are going to do.

17. I love how you practice preaching all day long. People think you are talking to yourself, but you are okay with that.

18. I love your helpfulness. You are willing and available to help me with anything and everything, even this list of compliments.

19. I love that you are a gentleman. You always rush ahead to open doors for me and others.

20. I love being your queen. You have declared me the queen to our children.

21. I love your generosity when it comes to my expensive tastes and hobbies. Whether it be cooking or designing, you love equipping me with the tools I "need" to do the job.

22. I love how you tolerate our dog, Sparkle. I know you are not a dog person. But you now enjoy her because I am a dog person. It is a major inconvenience to travel with her in the car, but you let her ride on your lap because of me.

23. I love that you are my number one taste tester. You love my cooking. Even when I ask for feedback on an unsuccessful dish, you find a way to point out the good stuff. Here, too, is where your skillful exaggeration comes in.

24. I love celebrating holidays with you. It takes days to set up our house, but when it is finished, you love turning on the lights each morning and relaxing in our home.

These lists are the lyrics of our duet. We sing them every day. One day, with hard work and plenty of jamming sessions, we will release our greatest hits. I want to sing these words over her at birthday parties, family reunions, special meals out, Thanksgiving meals, and anniversaries. I sing them to my kids, parents, congregation, friends, and total strangers.

When Carson and Corynn heard about these lists, they started working on their own. They each have a list called "Why I Love

Having Parents That Love Each Other." To date, Corynn has ten reasons and Carson has five.

Corynn's list:

1. We all have a better life.
2. My dad is able to work while my mom watches us.
3. They both make my brother and me laugh.
4. I don't have to worry about my parents divorcing.
5. We are and always will be a family that loves each other.
6. My brother and I are raised correctly.
7. We all are able to do more things now than we would if my parents did not love each other.
8. My parents don't fight.
9. They both love me, and they make sure that I know it.
10. If I am sick or sad, they make me feel better.

Carson's list:

1. They take care of me and Corynn.
2. They take care of each other.
3. I get to make them laugh.
4. They get along.
5. They share money.

My prayer is that you begin honoring marriage and praising your love before family and friends.

The FLY Journal (#funlovingyou)

Are you ready to write the lyrics for your duet? It's time for you and your spouse to create your own Fun Loving You lists. Here are some starters. Be a banner of love over your spouse! Send out a tweet with one or two reasons why it is fun loving your spouse.

When we met, I knew immediately _____.

When we are with your family, I love how you ___ _____.

As a mom, I love how you _____.

As a dad, I love how you _____.

When we travel, I love when you _____.

When we play games, I love the way you _____.

When you meet a stranger, I love how you _____.

When one of our kids gets hurt, I love how you immediately _____.

I love the way you serve our church by _____.

I love your personality and the way you _____.

Chapter 4

The Daily Getaway

My lover is to me a cluster of henna blossoms
from the vineyards of En Gedi.
—Song of Songs 1:14

I had a mentor years ago tell me, "Ted, if you want to have a great marriage, prioritize a daily delay, a weekly withdrawal, and an annual abandon." That three-point outline burned into my brain and never left. Ten years later, Amy and I use this model to prioritize daily, weekly, and annual time alone.

As I study the Song of Songs, all three are in there. Solomon and the Shulammite woman prioritize quality couple time.

A daily getaway is quality time spent in and around your home. A weekly getaway is spent away from your home but in town. We call this a date. An annual getaway is quality time spent out of town. Prioritizing and planning all three transform a marriage.

Desire and attraction grow in marriage when you spend quality time together. I'm not talking a few minutes here and there every day. I'm talking hours, not minutes. The Shulammite woman desires Solomon's time: ***"While the king was at his table, my perfume spread its fragrance. My beloved is to me a sachet of myrrh resting between my breasts. My beloved is to me a cluster of henna blossoms from the vineyards of En Gedi"*** (Song 1:12–14).

En Gedi is a lush oasis on the western shore of the Dead Sea in the midst of a desert wilderness. The NET Bible commentary describes this oasis as a small paradise to those traveling through the harsh conditions of the desert:

> The surrounding region is hot and bleak; its dry sands extend monotonously for miles.... The lush oasis of En Gedi is the only sign of greenery or life for miles around. It stands out as a surprising contrast to the bleak, dry desert wilderness around it. In the midst of this bleak desert wilderness is the lush oasis in which indescribable beauty is found. The lush oasis and waterfall brings welcome relief and refreshment to the weary desert traveler.[1]

An oasis is a place of refreshment, relaxation, rejuvenation, and rest. I want my home to be En Gedi. It must be a place of welcomed relief and refreshment surrounded by a dry, bleak, and dying world. Building this sanctuary must start in our marriage, and then it can trickle down to the kids.

Our En Gedi begins by prioritizing marriage and eradicating the kid-centered home. According to Genesis 2:24, God created the bond between husband and wife to be stronger than the bond between parent and child: "That is why a man leaves his father and mother and is united to his wife, and they become one flesh." Children are a welcomed addition to the home, but they are not going to be with us forever.

You can ask my seven-year-old son, Carson, "What is your dad's definition of maturity based on Genesis 2:24?"

He will say, "I will not be with Mom and Dad forever, so I must plan accordingly."

My responsibility as a parent is to prepare my child to leave home as an adult, not on a journey to become one. An En Gedi home prioritizes four spiritual journeys for the health of the marriage and the future of the child.

The first spiritual journey is mine. I pass on to my spouse and children what I have on my heart. I am 100 percent responsible for my heart and this journey. My constant desire is to connect to Jesus as the boss and source of my life.

The second spiritual journey is Amy's. She is 100 percent responsible for her journey, and I am 0 percent responsible for this journey. That frees me up to serve her rather than to be her source. She is plugged into the source of life, and together we give each other the overflow.

The third spiritual journey is our marriage journey. The apostle Paul describes this journey as a profound mystery: "'For this reason a man will leave his father and mother and be united to his wife, and the two will become one flesh.' This is a profound mystery—but I am talking about Christ and the church. However, each one of you also must love his wife as he loves himself, and the wife must respect her husband" (Eph. 5:31–33).

It's the moment in a wedding ceremony when we light the unity candle. The groom tilts toward the center, his candle representing his spiritual journey. The bride has a candle symbolizing her spiritual journey. The unity candle represents the marriage journey. This journey models the gospel of Jesus for our children.

I love sharing with the bride and groom, "One day, you will have a bunch of little candles running around." That is the final journey of an En Gedi home.

The fourth spiritual journey of the home is your child's journey. Deuteronomy 6:4–7 clearly defines the priority of these journeys: "Hear, O Israel: The LORD our God, the LORD is one. Love the LORD your God with all your heart and with all your soul and with all your strength. These commandments that I give you today are to be on your hearts. Impress them on your children. Talk about them when you sit at home and when you walk along the road, when you lie down and when you get up." God is the boss and source. Our home submits to His authority. We are to love the Lord. Verse 6 says these truths are to be upon our hearts first; then we impress them on our kids.

When we prioritize the child's journey above our own or our marriage's, we circumvent God's design for the heart.

Dr. Bob Paul is a dear friend of mine and the copresident of the National Institute of Marriage. With this first spiritual journey, he taught me years ago the value of caring for one's own heart. Making sure that your heart is full of God's love and the words of Christ is always in the best interest of all parties involved, because you can't give what you don't have. When you keep in mind that God made you for relationships, you stop self-care from degenerating into selfishness. Why? Because you realize that you take care of yourself so that you have something to give to others.

Years ago I hosted a coronation ceremony in honor of Amy's spiritual journey in our home. I sat my five-year-old daughter down and explained how our home had room for only one queen and she was not her. I remember Corynn looking at me with eyes that said, "We'll see about that."

I serve Amy by guarding her time so she can be alone and become refreshed. One way I do this is by keeping the kids busy when Mom wants to take a nice long soak.

I am heavily invested in our master bathroom. We have a jetted soaking tub that empties our eighty-gallon hot water heater. Surrounding the tub are candles, bath salts, and a plethora of bubble bath soap. We have a bamboo shelf that stretches across the tub to hold a magazine, drink, and loofah. A chandelier hangs over the tub and provides perfect mood lighting. Amy has a bath pillow to rest her head and one of the most expensive, lush towels available. I couldn't afford a set, so the one towel is only for her to use. Hands off for the rest of the family.

Nothing brings me greater joy than playing with the kids and sending Amy away for a little rest and rejuvenation. She and I regularly look for ways to prioritize our individual journeys. I am so blessed with Amy. She often tells me, "Stay away and don't come home until you feel productive." She knows productivity is a huge value for me. Since our ministry and family schedule is anything but ordinary, she knows I go through spells where I don't feel like much is getting done. Productivity is part of my self-care. After a day of producing, it is then that I love coming home to rest and recharge with my family for the next day.

Jon Jenkins is a good friend who married his college sweetheart, Heather. Ten years in and three kids later, Jon was feeling worn out from the grind. Jon and I are in the same season of life, marriage, and family. Our kids are friends, so we know many details of each other's home.

One day during this time of exhaustion, Jon called me while sitting in his truck outside his house. I'll never forget his call.

"Ted, give me one good reason to walk in this house," Jon said in jest. "As soon as I walk in the door, Heather will hand me the kids and expect me to entertain them for the next four hours. To do anything else will show that I am a bad dad. I'm a good dad, but is it too much to ask for a little downtime from a hectic day?"

He went on to say, "I get that Heather is with the kids all day while I am at work, but our home is starting to feel more like shift work rather than a couple raising children." What an observation. My friend Rick Rigsby echoed this thought when he told me his home had a "bunch of crazies" running around in it.

Heather, like every hardworking mom on the planet, deserves downtime and a little En Gedi every day. Jon, like every dutiful dad on the planet, needs En Gedi too. What they were experiencing were the effects of a kid-centered home.

"Jon, do you guys spend any time alone at night?" I asked.

"We always intend to after the kids go to bed, but by that time we are too tired and mad to enjoy being together. We usually crash on the couch in silence."

I could have told him to suck it up and endure it for the next few years, but I felt his pain. Been there, done that. So I avoided the minisermon and instead asked my favorite question, "How's that working for you?" Okay, I stole that line from Dr. Phil, but it is a great line.

Jon answered my question by insisting, "That's life!"

"Really, Jon? You believe that there is nothing you can do to bring some balance to your life, marriage, and children?" I asked.

Jon and I are very much alike. We believed for a long time that you have to choose between life, marriage, and family. This story is from a long time ago, and the good news is we learned a few things with young kids. Choosing is not necessary. The secret is prioritizing.

Without offending our wives, Jon and I have spent much time together over the years trying to find freedom from the kid-centered home. We love our kids, and we love spending time with them. We're not trying to get out of parenting. Not at all. We want to enjoy married life and raise great kids. Our marriage and family thrive when siblings play together outside, work on individual projects, and spend time reading. Mom and Dad do not need to be involved in the activities of the children every second of the day.

Slow Down, Breathe Deep, and Build Margin

"The apostles gathered around Jesus and reported to him all they had done and taught" (Mark 6:30). They were running full steam in their ministry, giving reports to Him. "Then, because so many people were coming and going that they did not even have a chance to eat, he said to them, 'Come with me by yourselves to a quiet place and get some rest'" (v. 31). Jesus knew they needed to rest and refuel to avoid burnout.

Amy and I will never run out of opportunities to serve people. We have busy schedules just like you and your spouse. There will always be stuff on your desk left to do, and often one of the hardest things to do is leave a task unfinished and pick it up when you get back. But we must unplug from work and prioritize rest.

Jesus valued rest because His Father valued rest. "What good is it for someone to gain the whole world, yet forfeit their soul?" (Mark 8:36). Chasing the American Dream is exhausting. Earning a living for your family wears you out. En Gedi provides rest and a reconnection with your heavenly Father. Need more convincing? Jesus went on to say, "What can anyone give in exchange for their soul?" (v. 37).

Your soul is important. Discipline yourself to unplug from work to focus on meeting your needs and those of your spouse. Remove distractions, and focus your attention on each other.

One way Amy and I create distraction-free zones is with the tech-free drawer. Clear out a drawer in your laundry room or kitchen, and label it "Tech-Free." At least once a day, place all of your technology in the drawer. That includes every phone, iPod, iPad, TV remote, and mobile device. As I write this, I am convicted. I need to do a better job leading in this area.

When you first start using the tech-free drawer, you will notice signs of withdrawal setting in. But hang in there. These will last for only a few weeks before unplugging becomes a new habit. We lower the stress in our home by regularly shutting down the technology.

Getting away from gadgets and television quickly and easily allows us to slow down our lives and build more margin into our marriage.

Prioritize mealtimes at home. Ronald Reagan said, "All great change in America happens around the dinner table." Amen! This discipline breathes life into relationships. I set the table and do the dishes. Amy is an incredible chef. We spend between thirty to forty-five minutes eating as a family and end our time with family devotions. We read from books, memorize Scripture, and study our A-to-Z nature-series devotional cards.

After dinner, the kids clear the table. Amy and I enjoy a daily delay for a few minutes, sitting at the cleared table. Our marriage needs this slow-paced conversation. Sometimes we end up sitting there, kid-free, for over an hour. Some nights our conversation lasts fifteen to twenty minutes. Whatever the case, we make sure we have an uninterrupted fifteen to twenty minutes each day exclusively for each other.

When you go home at night, let your home be the place where you disconnect from the world and the grind of your job. Limit your social-media usage. Surfing Facebook keeps you connected physically, relationally, and emotionally to friends, work, and responsibilities. In turn, you wear down.

En Gedi builds desire and attraction in marriage. Prioritizing marriage, then family, will create a deep sense of longing. To prove it, look at where we are now compared to where we started in Song of Songs. The book started out with the Shulammite woman expressing her desire, attraction, and then deep insecurity. Once she and Solomon move toward exclusivity in compliments and quality time, she feels secure and strong in their commitment. The last three verses of chapter 1 speak words of high honor and display the security that is in their home:

> *How beautiful you are, my darling!*
> *Oh, how beautiful!*
> *Your eyes are doves.*
> *How handsome you are, my beloved!*
> *Oh, how charming!*
> *And our bed is verdant.*
> *The beams of our house are cedars;*
> *our rafters are firs. (vv. 15–17)*

She describes a place where they can be secure together. Making our home En Gedi is a priority for our marriage and family. Amy and I invest in our home as a getaway. We have spaces all around our home where she and I carve out time for each other in a distraction-free zone.

Is your home an En Gedi in the midst of the grind? The Shulammite woman and Solomon declare their home an oasis. It is a place where they prioritize their relationship and relax together.

How do you know if your home is functioning like a desert oasis? Here are a few questions to consider:

Do you and your spouse look forward to coming home?

Do you and your spouse feel refreshed when you leave or return to your home?

Does everyone pull his or her weight with chores and household duties so everyone can relax and unplug? A good motto to live by is "Family fun when the chores are done."

The FLY Journal (#funlovingyou)

Here are some conversation starters for your daily getaway (you don't have to do all of these in one night!):

1. What was the hardest part of your day?
2. What was the best part of your day?
3. If I played hooky tomorrow, I would _____.
4. At _____ o'clock today, I was ready to come home.
5. Did you daydream at work today? If so, what about?
6. What made you feel the most productive at work today?
7. What was your biggest distraction?
8. On the drive home, I listened to _____.
9. Did you talk to anyone interesting today?
10. If you could change one thing about your day, what would it be? Any words you would take back?
11. I think it would be fun if we took the kids _____ next weekend.
12. We haven't talked to _____ in some time; we should call and see how they are doing.
13. What did you dream about doing for a career when you were a kid?
14. If you knew you couldn't fail, what would you wake up tomorrow and do?
15. If I handed you a check for ten million dollars, what would you do tomorrow at 8:00 a.m.?

16. If your job let you work and live anywhere in the world, where would you choose to live and why?

17. Which president, living or dead, would you most like to have lunch with and why?

18. Who is one person throughout history you would most want to meet?

19. If you starred in a movie sequel, which movie would it be?

20. If you could be an extra on a television show, what scene would you want to "star" in?

21. If you could be on a game show, which one would you go on and why?

22. If you could write a cover story for any magazine, what magazine would you choose? What would your article focus on?

23. When we got married, what did you dream our life would be like in ten years?

24. If you had one dream for our marriage, what would it be?

25. On your day off this week, what is the one thing you would like to do together to create a memory?

26. If we could spend Christmas anywhere in the world, where would you want to go?

27. What could I do this week that would make you feel extraspecial?

28. What country or people group do you have the biggest heart for?

29. If we could raise one million dollars to help those in need, to whom would you give that money?

30. What people group, organization, cause, or mission would you most want to give to over the next twelve months?

31. How do you desire to serve others this year, either in the community or at church?

32. If you could be a part of changing someone's life this year, how would you do that?

33. Who is one person you want to influence in the next twelve months?

34. Who is one person you would like to seek counsel from over the next twelve months?

35. What is your biggest goal for our family this coming year?

36. What is one place you most want to take our children?

37. What is your dream for our parents?

38. What do you imagine our grandchildren or great-grandchildren will be like? If we had only one week a year with them, what would we do?

39. What do you want to get better at?

40. If you could change one thing about yourself physically, what would it be?

41. When you retire, what do you want people to say about your life?

42. What are some things you've always wanted to do but haven't done yet?

43. If someone made a reality show about our lives and followed us around with cameras every day, what would you want the viewers to see in our lives? Our family? Our marriage?

44. Describe the person you want to be five years from now.

45. As your number one fan, what can I do to cheer you on?

46. Do you want to make love tonight?

47. Can you give me two to three ideas of adding adventure to our foreplay?

48. Have you ever wanted to be more adventurous in our sex life?

49. What could I do to be a better listener?

50. When you share your heart with me, do you think I understand what you are saying? Why or why not?

51. What physical cues can I give you so you know I got it?

52. This will be a relaxing evening if we _____.

Chapter 5

The Weekly Getaway (Date Night Challenge)

Arise, my darling, my beautiful one, come with me.

—Song of Songs 2:10

At our church, doctrine is foundational. We believe in the inspiration of Scripture. We believe in the substitutionary atonement of Christ. We believe in the royal priesthood of the saints. We believe in date nights. Keep them holy!

A weekly withdrawal is a getaway outside of your home and requires planning, scheduling, time, and money. The daily delay prioritizes quality couple time in the form of a microdate. It creates an En Gedi environment in the home. The weekly withdrawal carves out extended time each week to a special spot somewhere in or around town.

In the Song of Songs, Solomon picks up the Shulammite woman for a date. They are not yet married, and he is pictured in a hurry to get her and take her away for the night. It is a scene of excitement and anticipation:

> *Listen! My beloved!*
> *Look! Here he comes,*
> *leaping across the mountains,*
> *bounding over the hills.*
> *My beloved is like a gazelle or a young stag.*
> *Look! There he stands behind our wall,*
> *gazing through the windows,*
> *peering through the lattice.*
> *My beloved spoke and said to me,*
> *"Arise, my darling,*
> *my beautiful one, come with me."* (Song
> 2:8–10)

According to this text, a date has three key components. First, there is anticipation. He stands behind the wall, looking forward to seeing her, hoping to catch a glimpse. And, no, he's not a Peeping Tom or a stalker. Second, he picks her up. Third, there is an invitation to get out of the house. He says, "Come with me."

I know the stereotype is that women do not like to be surprised, but I challenge that. What women love is planning for a getaway. When a husband calls home to say, "I am coming home to get you and I'm taking you out tonight," a wife's first thought is, *I wonder where we are going?*

I believe a husband's initiative trumps the fear of surprise. Knowing that he is thinking about and planning something special is enough for her to call and brag on him to friends.

Amy and I date multiple times a week. To be honest, I so prioritize lunch dates with my wife that my role as senior pastor suffers at times. I get requests often for coffee and lunch that I decline simply because I want to be with my wife. Church staff and members in the past took this personally, but it had nothing to do with them. It had everything to do with my marriage. Amy and I have our favorite two or three spots that are our go-to restaurants. We live for menu changes season to season. We enjoy small plates and great conversation. Lunch dates are just part of our regular dating. We qualify a date official when it lasts three to five hours.

The University of Virginia releases a study every year as part of the National Marriage Project. In 2011, the researches studied date night initiatives popping up all over the country. According to their research, they identified key components of date nights and quality couple time that lead to increased marital satisfaction. Here are the five keys to great married dating.

First, dating keeps lines of communication open. With mobile devices out in the car and great eye contact, a date allows for extended conversation. "Date nights may help partners and spouses to 'stay current' with each other's lives and offer one another support for meeting these challenges."[1] It is very important to guard your dates from deep, escalated conversation. Avoid hot-button topics; save those for daily delays or microdates.

Second, dating is the perfect time for couples to try something new. Let's go against the grain and break the routine of dinner and a movie. A regular date night gives couples the opportunity to try something brand-new: "Most couples experience a decline in relationship quality after a few years, partly because they become habituated to one another and are more likely to take one another, and their relationship, for granted.... Thus, date nights should foster this higher quality, especially insofar as couples use them to engage in exciting, active, or unusual activities."[2] Instead of another movie, go roller-skating, skeet shooting, rock climbing, or take a cooking class.

Third, dating rediscovers passion and sparks sexual intimacy. Over time, couples see a decline in romantic pursuits. "Insofar as date nights allow couples to focus on their relationship, to share feelings, to engage in romantic activities with one another, and to try new things, date nights may strengthen or rekindle that romantic spark that can be helpful in sustaining the fires of love over the long haul."[3]

Fourth, dating shows commitment to the marriage. It is a signal to children, family, and friends that says, "We take our marriage seriously." It also says, "Our time together is valuable." "Date nights may solidify an expectation of commitment among couples by fostering a sense of togetherness, by allowing partners to signal to one another—as well as friends and family—that they take their relationship seriously, and by furnishing them with opportunities to spend time with one another, to communicate, and to enjoy fun activities together."[4]

Fifth, dating gives couples extended periods to de-stress. It provides the perfect platform to remove stress and distractions: "Date nights may be helpful for relieving stress on couples, as they allow them to enjoy time with one another apart from the pressing concerns of their ordinary life."[5]

With all the benefits dating brings to married life, why in the world do so many couples neglect it? The two most common excuses for skipping date night are kids and money. I hear it all the time. Prioritizing dating requires decisions on how you spend your money the rest of the week.

It is also possible to enjoy reasonably priced dates while capable family and friends care for the kids. I asked my Facebook friends for help on this one. Here are some of their ideas for solving the child-care and resource challenge:

Julie: We did a date co-op when our kids were little with some of our friends. We swapped babysitting for each other so we could get some alone time. The kids thought it was a playdate for them!

We discovered the beauty of having lunch dates at the nicer places. The prices are usually much lower, the portion sizes are smaller, and you still get the fancy feeling. Sometimes, if the lunch thing doesn't work out, we will eat a light meal at home and then just share an appetizer and dessert at a restaurant.

Tricia: At-home dates, after the kids go to bed. Play board games, romantic dessert date with candles, snuggle by the fire, babysitting exchange with friends. Ten-dollar store challenge (see who can come up with the most creative gift), cook dinner together (new recipe).

Jammie: We don't have small children, but we go on many dates that don't cost a thing. Dreaming together at Barnes & Noble as we look at books and magazines about home building. Walking hand in hand at the Landing, talking about our days or upcoming week. We occasionally take a dessert date to Vintage Paris or CherryBerry, which doesn't cost much. Make your regular planned meal, but pull out the fine china and candles. There are so many things you can do without a financial hit!

Karl: I have four kids, so getting out is not easy. One thing we do is have a weekly at-home date night. We put the kids to bed or have the oldest watch the baby. Then we make stir-fry together. We eat it while watching *Smallville*.

Heidi: Look for babysitters who tithe their time. A couple of my daughters chose to babysit for free at times as a tithe to the Lord. Not only did the parents get blessed, but the Lord brought in funds for my girls in other ways.

Jason: Depending on your spouse's love language, some of my most successful married dates haven't cost a dime. Go for a drive or find an old "parking" spot to bring back sparks from the past. Spend the evening reigniting memories of falling in love. Good old-fashioned quality time is still the best date in my book. Pack a picnic dinner and create your own "dessert"!

Connie: Feed the kids and put them to bed early. Then have your own romantic candlelit dinner in the bedroom while playing strip poker. I don't think I have to describe the rest of the evening.

Karen: My husband and I spend time together after putting the kids to bed early. My husband calls it a "state" … stay-at-home date.

Vicky: We used to do our grocery shopping in towns that were at least a half hour from the house. That way we would kill two birds with one stone.

Ruth: We meet on our lunch hour with packed sandwiches while the kids are at school—cheap and no sitter.

Lisa: I know of at least ten singles who would be happy to sit at no cost, and that includes *me*!

You might want to become friends with Lisa on Facebook and plan your first or next date in Branson. If not, I'm sure there are plenty of Lisas who care for kids on a regular basis in your neighborhood or church. It's time to adopt some parents and grandparents.

Did you catch the themes in those posts? Child-swapping dates, lunch dates, and "after the kids go to bed" dates seem to be the most popular.

The Case for Exclusivity in Dating and Marriage

Desire says, "I want you." Exclusivity says, "I want only you." This is the secret to a great marriage. Exclusivity is the essence of biblical marriage. Dating signals exclusivity.

In junior high we called this "going steady." You pledged your love to one person, and although you couldn't drive or go anywhere, you were exclusive to that person. So cute. In high school it changed. You "went out" as a sign of exclusivity. It usually included giving her your class ring or letterman's jacket. Married dating is different. It is a regular reminder to you, me, and those around us that these two go together. They are one.

Amy and I recently took a quick overnight trip to Colorado Springs. We love renting movies on the iPad for flights. When we combine speaking trips with romantic getaways, we always rent a romantic comedy. On this trip, we rented a dud. When it was over, I leaned over to Amy and said, "Well, that's two hours of my life I'm never going to get back." It was a horrible movie that should've been categorized in the horror genre. Do you know why? It was a trendy love movie with a depressing message. The whole point of this two-hour movie was, "I want to keep my options open. I don't want to get too serious." The main character loved the term *casual*. "Let's just keep this loose. Let's not define this."

There was nothing romantic about the movie. There is no romance in "keeping your options open." I don't choke up or tear up over independence. I was bored. I was sad. I was down in the dumps by the end of the movie.

As sappy, cheesy, and corny as it may sound, I love the scene where a guy and gal are standing face-to-face and she says something to him like, "I choose you. I want only you." Those are the good lines. That's why I love *Braveheart*. William Wallace sets out on a campaign to free his country. Where did his passion come from? His love for his wife!

The "keep it loose, casual, and open" theme does not work. There is no intimacy in casual, uncommitted love. This is where Song of Songs 2 begins.

In chapter 1, the Shulammite woman is explaining her insecurity about her body and her family. She has no idea why Solomon would choose her. She doesn't get it. She believes she is unattractive and nothing special.

As the book progresses and they approach the day of their wedding, she says, *"I am a rose of Sharon, a lily of the valleys"* (2:1). She declares that she is a common wildflower. In southwest Missouri we would call this the daffodil. In early March, these yellow wildflowers spring up everywhere. In other words, she is saying, "I am common. I'm nothing special. Why would you want to be with me? Why would you want to spend time with me? Why do you feel that I'm beautiful?"

He answers her with, *"Like a lily among thorns is my darling among the young women"* (v. 2). He speaks back to her and declares that he will be a one-woman man. He is saying, "Yeah, there are a lot of women out there to choose from, but I've chosen you." That's exclusivity.

Exclusivity makes a choice. When a man declares exclusive love toward a woman, security automatically happens. There may be other women to choose from, but I choose you. I want only you.

The Shulammite woman says, *"Like an apple tree among the trees of the forest is my beloved among the young men"* (v. 3). When she sees him, he is nourishment in the forest. He stands out. I'm going to get all worked up as I get into this, because I have all sorts of notes with stars by them, saying, "Don't miss this point."

She continues, *"I delight to sit in his shade, and his fruit is sweet to my taste."* She dwells, remains, and abides in him. Her desire is to spend a lot of slow-paced time with him. Solomon protects and provides for her because *"he has brought me to his banquet hall, and his banner over me is love"* (v. 4 NASB). He has taken her to a house of feasting, a place where there is wine and relaxation.

Warfare in Solomon's day was hand-to-hand combat. On the sides of the battlefield, each army hoisted a banner. As the battle raged, the banner was the rallying point. Soldiers regrouped around the banner. There was safety in numbers. The banner meant reinforcements and protection. Solomon is the Shulammite woman's banner. When she rallies around him, she is safe. In other words, "When I'm with him, I feel safe; when I'm with him, I feel secure."

I get that I'm not Red Lobster's fresh catch of the day. One look at my picture on the back cover of this book and you will quickly realize that I am not Jack Bauer, Chuck Norris, or Jean-Claude Van Damme. I'm a type A personality but a far cry from a battle-ready warrior. However, that does not matter. I am Amy Cunningham's warrior. When we go to a restaurant, I position myself to know what is going on in the room. If something were to break out, I've got my plan. I am constantly looking around the room. Then I almost get to the point where I hope something does go down. I always like to keep my eye on the door in case some crazy guy comes in. I do the same thing at airports and on planes. If something like that happens, I have the logistics worked out in my head. If I can't save her, I am going to die trying.

Here is where the feminist movement took a wrong turn. When a man protects and provides for a woman, it does not mean that the woman is weak. Just the opposite. Amy is an extremely confident and strong woman. She is no weakling. But she loves letting me protect her. It turns her on.

Solomon provides protection, and it gets steamy. His lover says, *"Strengthen me with raisins, refresh me with apples, for I am faint with love. His left arm is under my head, and his right arm embraces me"* (2:5–6). Protection is an aphrodisiac. It heightens desire. This woman is lovesick. Her heart is pitter-pattering. Exclusivity sparks sexual desire.

This is the opposite of what the world teaches. The world says, "You want to increase frequency in your sex life? Then view pornography. The best way to increase drive is to entice each other with erotica."

Great, fresh, and fun sex does not come from viewing pornography. Great sex flows from exclusivity. One man, one woman, for one lifetime. Pastor Mark Gungor taught me how to prove that exclusivity, not pornography, creates sexual desire.

I used Pastor Mark's assessment one Sunday at Woodland Hills during a marriage message. I asked the wives of our congregation if they would be open to helping me with the research. They obliged.

I asked, "Ladies, would you please raise your hand if you are okay with your husband thinking about someone else while he makes love to you?"

As I looked around, not one hand went up. "Okay, we are going to call that zero.

"Let me ask you this. Raise your hand if you want to be the only one he thinks about while making love to you," I requested. As hands went up, I said, "Please keep them up; we are doing research."

Looking over the congregation, I said, "We are going to call that a bunch."

It is not scientific, but it makes the point. Women desire exclusivity in sexual intimacy.

As exclusivity peaks for Solomon and the Shulammite woman, a caution goes out: ***"Daughters of Jerusalem, I charge you by the gazelles and by the does of the field: Do not arouse or awaken love until it so desires"*** (2:7). Love has a pace and rhythm. As her desire for Solomon grows, they guard themselves by slowing the pace. But this is a very important point: they do not halt the pace of desire; they halt at the threshold of physical intimacy. Sexual intimacy is reserved for the exclusivity of marriage.

Exclusivity, longevity, and lifetime are synonymous in marriage. Exclusivity makes the choice to give up all other choices. It decides to burn every bridge with the opposite sex, unfriend every temptation on Facebook, and sever ties with flirtatious encounters.

Exclusivity linked with anticipation pictures a special future for your marriage. Amy and I spend a lot of time on our dates talking about the future. We love forward thinking. It breathes life into our marriage and gives us something to look forward to. That is perfect dating—looking forward to dates to look forward to the future.

When I think of anticipation, Thanksgiving and Christmas come to mind. Thanksgiving is a day of anticipation. Christmas is a season of anticipation. On Thanksgiving Day, we smell the meal all day. It is easy to wait because we know we will enjoy the food later that same day. Not always true with Christmas. Maybe your parents were cruel and placed the presents under the tree weeks before December

25. Cruel! My kids can't stand that delay. I remind them, "It builds character."

Anticipation heightens marital enjoyment. Amy and I look forward to vacations, special church services, back-to-school experiences, trips, conferences, dates, birthdays, weekends, get-togethers, book releases, chiropractor appointments, and bedtime (the kids' and ours). We always have something to look forward to. This is a key ingredient to keeping marriage fresh and fun.

Whatever season of life your marriage is in, you need to date as a constant reminder of what you have to look forward to.

Every September around our church, I see the sadness on the moms' faces who sent their last child off to college. Amy regularly reminds me that humor is not a good pastoral strategy for encouraging such moms.

Sonya Hayter, the wife of one of our elders, sent her youngest off to college last year. The first time I asked her about it, she couldn't say a word. She was *verklempt*.

"Sonya, are you okay?" I asked. The tears immediately formed. She wouldn't speak a word. I had one-liners ready to easy her pain, but I bit my tongue. I kept them all inside.

One Sunday morning in November, Sonya sought me out and said, "Ted, I just wanted to tell you I'm healed. Life is good." Her smile was ear to ear. She was enjoying this new season with her husband, Doug. They date multiple times a week.

There are always new seasons to anticipate. Life is full of transitions. College to career. Independence to marriage. Honeymoon to home. Newlywed to baby. Baby to multiple kids. Toddlers to teens. Kids to empty nest. Empty nest to retirement.

Can you picture your next season? What are you looking forward to in that season?

Anticipation pictures a special future by planning. The best part is you may never see the plans come to full fruition, but there is great value in the planning. Dreaming is a lost art for couples.

Do you and your spouse dream together? Amy and I usually do our best dreaming on dates after we have removed all distractions. We use that time to plan our next seasons of life. We discuss trips we want to go on, some of which are years out. We picture a special future for our kids and church. This is a great mental exercise that breathes life into marriage.

If your kids are all in high school right now, you need to think about how special it's going to be when they are gone. Those crazies won't be with you forever.

You may be in the toddler or infant season. Do yourself a favor and buy a playpen. You may already have one, but you call it a portable crib. Get it out, and set your child in it with a toy or two. That gives you a few moments to break away from the grind at home to talk marriage planning. Kids drain a marriage if Mom and Dad allow it. You need regular times of conversation to picture and plan a special future.

Whenever I share the playpen illustration at conferences, the people from the builder generation (those born before 1946) laugh the hardest because they remember using them. It was a primary tool in allowing parents to get housework done and spend time together. Baby boomers (those born between 1946 and 1962) laugh as well because they remember entertaining themselves in them. I ask at every conference, "Does anyone remember when you started crawling out of the playpen and Mom and Dad turned it upside down to contain you?" At least twelve people raise their hands, and everyone laughs. The point is we all relate to coddling our kids to the point of a suffering marriage.

Amy and I don't want to be that couple at Cracker Barrel who sits there speechless for an hour and half slurping soup. There is no fun in listening to your spouse eat. The practice of dreaming and picturing a special future is for right now. When we are in our seventies, I want Amy and me to have conversations like this: "Hey, I know we're seventy, but what's next? Where are we going special? What are we going to do? What do you want to do with the grandkids when they come over? Where could we do a family reunion? Is there anything special you want to change around the house? Any new restaurants you want to try?"

I love my business-minded friends. They are great at planning for business and career but often never give planning in marriage a second (or first) thought. Bring your strategic planning skills to your dating and marriage. Write out a plan. Revisit the plan every few months and look at your WIN list. WIN stands for "what's important now." Adjust your plans as you dream together.

Amy and I lost this art after a few years of marriage, but now we do it like crazy. Now we have big plans! A lot of our plans are very expensive and may never happen. That's perfectly okay. The value is not always in the execution. We have plans around our house. We love dreaming around the home improvement store. We have an amazing backyard-entertaining space planned but may or may not get around to it. We have a make-believe list that we refer to when planning.

I ask, "What number is the fire pit?"

Amy responds, "Number 472."

I ask, "What about the shed?"

She says, "Number 189."

I know the answer when I ask, "What about a golf cart?" Its place on our list is always in flux.

She says, "Number 7,831." It's almost off the list entirely. But you never know. We may need it to get the mail in our seventies. I'm holding out.

Anticipation builds on exclusivity. Once committed for life, you have the security to make plans. Anticipation is pictured as springtime in the Song of Songs. Solomon is seen chasing after the Shulammite woman. He is running. He is excited. His actions say, "I want to be with her. I want to spend time with her." They spend time together on a special night out.

She says, *"Listen! My beloved! Look! Here he comes, leaping across the mountains, bounding over the hills. My beloved is like a gazelle or a young stag. Look! There he stands behind our wall, gazing through the windows, peering through the lattice"* (2:8–9). In essence he is saying, "I see her, but I'm not yet with her." He is not walking. He is not skipping. The scripture says he is "leaping." He is approaching quickly. He is excited. He wants to be with her. He is bounding over the hills.

Maybe I am taking this text too literally, or perhaps I am too traditional in my thinking, but I think there is a strong application here. In fact, I see two subtle applications.

First, the young man is pursuing the woman. I love that. My advocacy for young people dating, falling in love, and marrying gets me in hot water, especially with parents. In my book *Young and in Love* I challenge the unnecessary delay of marriage. Young people have delayed marriage to prioritize college, career, money, independence, and travel. *Again, independence* is a socially acceptable term for selfishness. We need pastors and parents to be marriage advocates. We need to be the loudest voices saying, "Love and marriage are from our Lord. They are good things. Go after them. Do not make marriage an afterthought in the adult milestones. Move it up on the list. Young men, start asking women out." See, that's why I get into so much trouble.

Second, you'll notice that Solomon goes to her house. My daughter is nine. She is not dating yet. I don't have many rules in our home, but the young man picking her up from our house is going to be one of them. No meeting at the movies or mall. I want to get to know him. I want to look into his eyes and see deep into his soul. Not to scare him, but to get to know him. Okay, maybe just a little scare.

The same thing goes for my son. Carson needs to go and meet the parents. Spending time with parents serves two purposes: they get to see what they and their daughter are getting into, and you get to see what you are getting into.

To this day, sixteen years into marriage, I love picking up Amy for a date. Married couples have an advantage in dating. We are allowed a sneak peek while getting ready for the date. I love watching my wife get ready for a date. I love when she takes her time. Knowing you have a special time planned in the evening can also make the workday go fast.

The Shulammite woman continues with the word picture of spring and says, **"My beloved spoke and said to me, 'Arise, my** *darling, my beautiful one, come with me. See! The winter is past; the rains are over and gone. Flowers appear on the earth; the season of singing has come, the cooing of doves is heard in our land. The fig tree forms its early fruit; the blossoming vines spread their fragrance. Arise, come, my darling; my beautiful one, come with me'"* (2:10–13).

Winter is a tough season for me. I struggle with a mild case of SAD (seasonal affective disorder). This is not an official diagnosis, but every January, after weeks of cloudy skies and cold temperatures, I need the sun. I need the warmth. Fortunately, I serve on the teaching team at Mission Community Church in Gilbert, Arizona. People sometimes stare at me when they see me standing on the blacktop in the parking lot of the church on a ninety-plus-degree day with my eyes closed and head pointed toward the sun. I'm soaking up the rays and heat.

Fresh is best understood in the transition from winter to spring. Budding trees, greening grass, chirping birds, and longer days set the backdrop for a new season. This is the best part of living in the Ozark Mountains. We enjoy all four seasons in equal parts. They each seem to get three months a year.

Is your marriage in a winter season? Cold? Dark? What will it take to bring you into spring? Dating is the perfect way to bring your marriage out of a cold snap.

One very important aspect of dating is curiosity and fascination. A date is the perfect time to dig a little deeper and discover something about your spouse.

My daughter is a nature nut. She loves the great outdoors. Spring is her favorite season. She loves picking up the rocks and boulders in our landscape to discover creepy crawlies. There's everything you can imagine living in our yard. We live out in the sticks, and there are creatures galore. She finds momma snakes, baby snakes, frogs, toads, slugs, snails, geckos, momma lizards, and baby lizards. We keep them as pets for the day and release them at night right before bedtime.

Corynn loves hiking through our tick-infested side woods. If she sees something moving, she darts over to check it out. I once was about twenty steps behind when she took off running down a path. I saw her jump over something but was unable to identify the object until I got closer. It was a five-foot-long momma snake coiled on the path. My heart sank into my stomach. When I told her what she unknowingly did, she said, "Let's go see what kind it is." She plays with the nonvenomous snakes and avoids the copperheads and cottonmouths. Nice.

Curiosity says, "I want to discover something new." Discovery is not afraid to get dirty and pick up a rock or two to find something new. You must constantly be learning and discovering your spouse.

Children love discovery. Part of childlike curiosity is their non-stop question asking. They do not accept things at face value; they want to know why and how something works the way it does. As a parent, there is a universal answer to every question: "Because." Use *because* enough, and your kids will stop asking questions. You don't need all the answers, but an honest attempt at the answer keeps your kids guessing. It keeps them curious.

Do you suffer from a "because" marriage? As we grow, age, and move on in marriage, we reach a point where we feel like we've learned enough. Curiosity is drained from the marriage. When we observe something new in our spouse, instead of asking great questions to discover more, we kick back and tell ourselves, "Because."

Not only was Solomon curious about the Shulammite woman, but he also desired to draw her out: ***"My dove in the clefts of the rock, in the hiding places on the mountainside, show me your face, let me hear your voice; for your voice is sweet, and your face is lovely. Catch for us the foxes, the little foxes that ruin the vineyards, our vineyards that are in bloom"*** (2:14–15). Foxes kill curiosity. Guys, you may be thinking, *Yeah, but we already know each other. We spend plenty of time together. I finish her sentences for her, and she finishes mine.* That thinking is like the fox. It creates a vacuum of intimacy and kills the marriage. Guys, draw her out and kill the fox.

Solomon is saying, "I want to get to know you." He loves it when she speaks and shares herself with him. He wants to communicate with her. Dating is all about *curiosity* and *fascination*, spending countless hours getting to know each other. Ask great questions, diving deep into the heart of each other.

Marriage requires *duty* and *responsibility*. The key is not to replace curiosity and fascination with duty and responsibility. We must balance them all. Dating will help you find and keep that balance. My wife did not fall in love with me because of my job or the fact that I was great at mowing the lawn, but because I got to know her. She felt what Solomon's beloved felt: ***"My beloved is mine and I am his; he browses among the lilies. Until the day breaks and the shadows flee, turn, my beloved, and be like a gazelle or like a young stag on the rugged hills"*** (vv. 16–17). They give to each other. They are part of each other. Exclusivity in marriage means "I am yours; you are mine."

Their dating and exclusivity increase sexual desire. No better way for a married couple to end date night than with extended lovemaking. However, the date doesn't start in the bedroom. You end up there after an evening of asking each other great questions.

Continue to ask each other great questions to get to know each other deeply. Keep a regular date night free from distraction. Revisit some of the places you frequented on your first dates. If they are too far away, reminisce about your favorite restaurants, past vacations, honeymoon spot, and so on.

The FLY Journal (#funlovingyou)

The Date Night Challenge

The challenge is simple. Plan four dates in the next four weeks. Each date has a theme: play, laugh, dream, and adventure. For each date, I want to give you ten date ideas and fifty-two conversation starters.

You determine the when, where, and how much. The activity is up to you. Once you plan the date, use the fifty-two questions to probe deep into the heart of your spouse. My friend Joshua Straub is the date night challenge Jedi master at our church. He worked with me in creating these date ideas and questions. He and I both use these date ideas and questions on a regular basis.

Woodland Hills Family Church would love to keep up with and encourage your dating. Share your ideas and dates with us. I would love to see *Fun Loving You* readers interact on Twitter with #funlovingyou. Tweet your dates and pictures, when appropriate.

PLAYDATE: Enjoying time together without serious discussion
DATEIDEAS

1. Create a love playlist: You remember love tapes? You would record your favorite music on a cassette tape and give it to the one you were dating. Download your favorite love songs, and create a playlist called "Love playlist." It needs to have at least four or five songs. Don't stop with one playlist. Create a list from each decade. You can date the playlists or even create new playlists for special occasions. After you create the playlist, take a drive. Enjoy the sights of your town with the windows rolled down and the tunes cranked up.

2. Plan a picnic. Fill a basket or cooler with bread, goodies, cheese, fruit, drinks, etc. Grab a blanket and head to a park or lake.

3. Go to a coffee shop and take your own board games. Play checkers, cards, etc., while having coffee or tea together.

4. Visit a zoo, aquarium, museum, or botanical garden.

5. Choose a favorite activity from your junior or senior high days. Bowling, roller-skating, miniature golf, go-karts, etc. Also, trampoline places (e.g., Gravity Park) are popping up all over the country for those of you who don't have one in your backyard.

6. Cook a multicourse meal. Play with various recipes, and serve one course at a time. A great way

to have fun with this is to prepare a five-course meal together with drinks. This will be a long meal. Make it as formal as you'd like or as informal and goofy as you'd like.

7. Go fishing on the weekend. This is a great date whether you catch fish or not.

8. To add some random fun to your evening, go to a karaoke bar, and sing your favorite songs as loud as you can with people you've never met before.

9. Go on a picture date. Find random sites and take pictures of each other. To add more fun to it, make a theme around your pictures. For instance, go out as a tourist. Or go out together as if you were living in the 1950s, dress the part, hit a diner, and take fun pictures. You could also go as outdoorsy folks and take pictures in Bass Pro Shops or wearing camouflage.

10. Decide on a new hobby or activity together and begin practicing. For instance, you may decide you're going to run a 10k or a marathon together. Start running together to train for it. Perhaps you're wanting to learn an instrument together. Sign up, and begin taking lessons and practicing together.

PLAY52

1. On a scale of 1 to 10, how would you rate our "playtime" together?

2. How are you feeling the grind of life this week?

3. What parts of your job are the most tedious and exhausting?

4. How long does it take you each night to unwind physically, emotionally, and relationally from work?

5. What are some escape mechanisms we use in the midst of the grind?

6. Why does play feel irresponsible to adults?

7. If I can't enjoy life, I can't enjoy my spouse. What can I do today to better appreciate and enjoy life? (This is a personal question, not a marriage question.)

8. We need to spend ___ hours a week playing together.

9. If we have only twenty minutes to play, what should be our go-to activity?

10. What one leisure activity do you wish I would do with you more often?

11. Are there barriers to "play" that have been preventing us from having fun together (e.g., attitudes, lack of similar interests, laziness, work schedule, kids, etc.)?

12. What are some creative ways of overcoming these barriers to increase play in our relationship?

13. Are there attitudes or behaviors you see in me that make certain activities we do together unenjoyable for you (e.g., married to cell phone, poor attitude, etc.)?

14. What is the most frustrating thing I do when we try to do an activity together?

15. What one activity do you dislike doing that I really enjoy?

16. What could we do together to make that activity more enjoyable for you?

17. What is your best memory of a time we "played" together?

18. What one recreation do you most wish we would do together if we could do anything at all?

19. Is there a particular hobby you wish we could take up together?

20. Do you feel more satisfied by planned leisure activities or by spontaneous adventures?

21. What activities make you feel most loved?

22. What can I do to make leisure together more enjoyable for you?

(Spontaneous Play)

23. What makes being spontaneous difficult for us?

24. How could we build some more spontaneity into our daily or weekly routine?

25. What's the best memory you have of being spontaneous together?

26. Would you be willing to play or walk in the rain together?

27. Going skinny-dipping together would be _____
_____.

28. What concerns would you have about dropping everything for a two- to three-day unplanned

road trip out of town together, planning as we go?

(Daily Play)

29. Where in our daily routine do we have the most time for play?

30. What are some ways we could turn everyday household chores into a playful time together?

31. How could we add or combine an exercise or fitness regiment where we're working out together a few times a week?

32. What activities do we currently do apart that we could start doing together more often (e.g., grocery shopping, cooking together, working out, etc.)?

33. What are some creative ways we could redesign our house together?

34. Is there yard work, landscaping, or gardening we could do together?

35. What hobby or activity do we have the most common interest in?

36. How could we implement that activity into our daily lives?

(Intentional Play)

37. On a scale of 1 to 10 how satisfied are you with how intentional I am at planning leisure activities?

38. What are some ways we can be more intentional at making playtime happen in our relationship?

39. What is your favorite season of the year for leisure activities?

40. If you were to create a bucket list of twelve activities or playtime experiences for the next year, what would you include?

41. What are three activities you have done that you'd love for me to try?

42. What do you think about planning a camping trip together this summer?

43. What are some memories we could create together by stretching each other's skills and interests (e.g., teaching your husband to decorate, taking your wife along with you golfing, etc.)?

44. Are there any sports you would enjoy playing or getting more involved in together?

45. What is an act of kindness or charity you could do for your neighbors?

46. What is your ideal night out?

47. What are your five most favorite restaurants?

48. What are your five most favorite desserts?

49. What are your five most favorite indoor recreational activities (e.g., movies, laser tag, karaoke, bowling, etc.)?

50. What are your five most favorite outdoor recreational activities (e.g., hiking, fishing, miniature golf, swimming, etc.)?

51. How do you feel about setting a goal together that will require playtime in order to accomplish that

goal (e.g., training for and running a race together, taking dance lessons, taking a cooking class, etc.)?

52. How could we spice up that particular room to make it more playful?

LAUGHDATE: Learning to lighten up and not take ourselves too seriously

DATEIDEAS

1. Have a YouTube date. Spend an hour on YouTube watching great videos that will make you laugh. Here are a few to get you started:

> www.youtube.com/watch?v=yR0lWICH3rY
> www.youtube.com/watch?v=RP4abiHdQpc
> www.youtube.com/watch?v=NAFiU6bZ678
> www.youtube.com/watch?v=mIMFL9wRaJE

2. Meet for lunch, or go to a coffee shop or somewhere you enjoy being together. Bring the Laugh52 questions, and share stories with each other.

3. What's your favorite comedy of all time? Rent that movie for old times' sake, and stay home together and laugh. You could even rent a holiday comedy out of season (*Elf, Christmas Vacation,* etc.).

4. Book tickets to see a comedian coming to the area.

5. Set a date night either together or with other couples and play "Whose Line Is It Anyway?" You can find a list of the games from the TV show by simply doing a Google search of the show. Have fun with the ad-libs all night long.

6. Take a mini–road trip and do karaoke in the car. Sing your favorite songs as loud as you can. Sing the greatest duets of all time. Here are five of Billboard's top duets of all time:

> #35: "I Got You Babe" (1965) Sonny and Cher
> #31: "I Knew You Were Waiting (For Me)" (1987) Aretha Franklin and George Michael
> #26: "(I've Had) The Time of My Life" (1987) Bill Medley and Jennifer Warnes
> #9: "Islands in the Stream" (1983) Kenny Rogers and Dolly Parton
> #1: "Endless Love" (1981) Diana Ross and Lionel Richie[6]

7. Find an activity neither one of you are that good at and attempt it together. For instance, you could go roller-skating, ice-skating, kayaking, tandem biking, etc.

8. Take out the old yearbooks or annuals. Go through and laugh at yourself. Your dress, hairstyle, etc. Categorize and rank them. Ugliest hairdo. Most gaudy dress.

9. Sign up for a dance lesson. The dance instructor determines the level of fun. If he or she is overly strict and serious, that gives less seasoned dancers something to laugh about. This date will force you out of your comfort zone.

10. Spend one hour at an arcade. After you get over your anger at the price of games these days, try some of the physical games (dancing, basketball shooting, Skee-Ball, strength games). You'll get a laugh out of the competitive spirit that rises up in you.

LAUGH52

1. In what ways do I take myself too seriously?
2. Is there a vacuum of laughter in our home?
3. In what areas of life do I need to lighten up?
4. Practice and deliver a one-liner from a famous comedian (this may take some time in front of the mirror rehearsing before the date). Here are some to get you started:

> "Women don't want to hear what you think. Women want to hear what they think—in a deeper voice." —Bill Cosby
>
> "I don't like country music, but I don't mean to denigrate those who do. And for the people who like country music, *denigrate* means 'put down.'" —Bob Newhart

"Changing a diaper is a lot like getting a present from your grandmother—you're not sure what you've got but you're pretty sure you're not going to like it." —Jeff Foxworthy

"I took a speed reading course and not to brag but my speed shot up to forty-three pages a minute. But my comprehension plummeted." —Brian Regan

5. Think back to when you were in elementary school. What is the funniest experience you remember?

6. When was the last time you laughed so hard you cried?

7. Who is the funniest person you've ever met?

8. What is the craziest thing you ever did in a store?

9. When was the last time you tripped and fell in front of others?

10. Name the most embarrassing thing that's happened to you in the last year.

11. What is the funniest movie you've ever seen?

12. What is the most embarrassing thing you've ever done while playing with our kids?

13. What is the fastest way to make our kids laugh?

14. What makes you laugh the hardest?

15. What's the funniest thing I've ever said to you?

16. What is the funniest thing you've ever seen me do?

17. What is the grossest thing you've ever eaten?

18. When was the last time I really made you laugh?

19. Fill in the blank: I'm most fun to be around when I _____.

20. What is the funniest thing you've ever heard our kids say?

21. When was the last time you had to bite your lip to keep from laughing?

22. What do you do or think about to keep from laughing at an inappropriate time?

23. Name the last time you laughed at a really inappropriate time.

24. Name the last time you busted out laughing after watching a stranger.

25. Looking back at pictures from your younger days, what was the most embarrassing hairstyle you sported?

26. What's the most embarrassing outfit you've ever been caught wearing?

27. If you weren't worried about what other people thought, what is the one thing you wish you could do in public?

28. If you knew no one would see you, what dance would you do down the aisles of a store?

29. What's your favorite but most embarrassing dance move?

30. Have you ever left the house forgetting to put on an important article of clothing?

31. Name one song or movie you love but are embarrassed to admit.

32. When was the last time you were genuinely scared about something that turned out to be absolutely harmless?

33. What is the most embarrassing thing you've had to buy at a store?

34. Is there one photo of yourself that you laugh at every time you see it?

35. What's the silliest thing you remember us doing together?

36. What's the funniest license plate or bumper sticker you've ever seen?

37. Name the funniest thing you remember happening in church.

38. If you didn't have to act your age for a day, what kid-like things would you love to do?

39. Have you ever laughed or wanted to laugh while watching me sleep?

40. If you're having a bad day, what can I do to make you laugh?

41. What word do you think is just weird?

42. What's the most embarrassing gift you ever received but had to pretend you liked it?

43. When you were in high school, what did you wear that made you feel supercool but now is just embarrassing?

44. When was the last time the kids embarrassed you in public by something they said or did?

45. Have you ever sent a text or email to someone else that was supposed to go to me?

46. What's your funniest Christmas memory?

47. When was the last time we had a disagreement that ended in us laughing at ourselves?

48. When was the last time you saw a couple wearing matching outfits? Have we ever done that?

49. If I'm grumpy, what's one thing you try to do to snap me out of it?

50. When you _____, I can't help but smile.

51. Name something your parents said on a regular basis that drove you crazy but now makes you smile.

52. What's the most embarrassing thing you ever saw your parents do?

DREAMDATE: Picturing a special future for your marriage and family
DATEIDEAS

1. Walk down memory lane. Bust open those yearbooks and wedding albums. Discuss old friends, classes, favorite teachers, sports, and clothing. And don't forget to admire those hairstyles. What do you miss about those days? What do you miss least? If you could go back, what would you change?

2. Have a coronation date. Honor each other with the royal treatment. What does your spouse enjoy most? A back rub? Uninterrupted listening? A favorite movie? A favorite meal? Your answer to that question determines what you do on your date. Note: this date is actually two in one since each of you gets a turn receiving the royal treatment.

3. Plan an annual abandon. Even though it may be years away, plan that trip you've always dreamed of taking. Magazines and travel websites will help with the planning. Once your budget is set, put a plan in place together to start saving the money to take your dream trip.

4. Take a day and go house hunting. Look around at various homes, dream together, and make fun of the way others decorate.

5. Go to a coffee shop together after dinner, and take the Dream52 questions along with you. With a piece of paper, begin writing down the achievable dreams you want to begin pursuing for your marriage and family. After you have come up with an agreed-upon list of answers, start putting on paper a plan to begin living out those dreams together.

6. Have dinner in Italy. Or any of your favorite cities or countries. Transport the dream location to your own home. Set up decor to match the locale,

dress as if you were in that city or country, and cook the native cuisine.

7. If there is a hobby or activity you have always wanted to try, use this date night to give it a whirl. If you have never been bowling and would like to learn, give it a try. If it's building large puzzles, sit together and assemble one. Perhaps you have never crocheted before but always wanted to learn how. Research it and get the materials together to do it.

8. Set up a horseback-riding adventure together, and have a picnic along your route.

9. What is the most inspiring movie you have ever watched? A movie that makes you dream and come alive? Rent this movie, and watch it together early in the evening. When you're finished with the movie, sit down together, and use the passion and energy you have from watching the movie to dream together about your future as a couple and family.

10. Sit down together, and make a list of everything you would love to do inside and outside your home to make it more of what you want. Begin researching building-supply stores to find out the costs of each item. You can also search blogs to find cheap ways to redecorate and refurnish your home. Research these blogs together, and use a date night to slowly begin a home makeover.

DREAM56

1. At this point in your life, which would you choose to make your life better: better physical health, better relationships, more money, or a different job?

2. If you could rewind to any point in your life, what would you want to relive? Would you enjoy it the same or change it?

3. What would you do if you didn't have to work?

4. What award would you like to win and for what achievement?

5. When do you feel most alive?

6. If you could try out any occupation for a year, what would it be?

7. How would you spend a perfect day alone?

8. Choose four vacations—all expenses paid, of course—for both of us to take. Each has a theme: most romantic, most fun, most adventurous, most relaxing. Where would you go for each?

9. What would you do with ten million dollars?

10. If you could take lessons to become an expert at anything, what would it be?

11. Hollywood called. They want to make a movie about us. What would it be about, and who would play each of us?

12. If you could be a professional athlete, regardless of age or physical ability, what sport do you think you would enjoy the most?

13. Describe your dream house.

14. If you could have dinner with three famous people, living or dead, who would they be?

15. Name something you love that no one else seems to like. Or, vice versa, name something everyone seems to love but you dislike.

16. Of the following adventures, which would you choose first and why: (a) snow skiing, (b) cheese-and-wine night, (c) spelunking, (d) movie night, (e) a pro sports event, or (f) camping?

17. If you could have one superhero power, what would it be?

18. Sing the chorus or one line of my favorite love song.

19. What's the greatest invention of our lifetime?

20. What TV sitcom family would you be a member of?

21. What is one item you know you should get rid of but never will?

22. What were your favorite toys as a child?

23. Where do you most enjoy sitting outside your house?

24. Name three countries you'd like to visit.

25. What celebrity annoys you most?

26. Describe your dream car.

27. What causes the most stress or conflict in your marriage: financial decisions, sexual expectations, parenting styles, value differences?

28. What positive thing do I not say enough to you?

29. What would we do for the next ten years if we knew they were going to be our last?

30. Name one way I make you feel secure.

31. Name one thing you miss about our dating relationship.

32. How would I describe you to a stranger?

33. What is the sweetest thing I have ever said to you?

34. If we had an entire day to spend alone with each other, how would we spend it?

35. Recall all the details of the marriage proposal.

36. What's the most romantic scene from a movie you can think of?

37. What is your perfect Valentine's Day date?

38. What's the most romantic season of the year?

39. How would you like people to describe you at your funeral?

40. Tell about an experience that was difficult but necessary in making you the person you are today.

41. What is your religious background? In what way has it affected you most?

42. If you wrote a book about your life, what would it be called?

43. What makes you most humble?

44. Name a song that you could really relate to at some point in your life.

45. What scares you most?

46. What is the most honest thing you have ever done?

47. What's the best advice someone ever gave you?

48. What makes you most uncomfortable: being around new people, formal occasions, speaking to a large group?

49. On a scale of 1 to 10, how "cool" are you?

50. Tell about a favorite childhood memory you made with your family.

51. Do you ever catch yourself dreaming about a life without me? What relationships, activities, or routines do we need to end today to begin building back dreams with each other?

52. What are two or three dreams we have for our empty-nest years? Where will we live? Where will we visit? How will we serve the church? What will our retirement years look like?

53. What dreams do we have for our kids?

54. How can we better prepare our kids for the world?

55. What are our children learning about hearts for the world?

56. What are a few areas in our home we can change to begin developing a deeper love and heart for the world?

ADVENTUREDATE: Trying something new and taking risks
DATEIDEAS

1. Do a 5k run, walk, or hike. You can break it up into one-mile increments, so long as you get in the

3.1 miles. This is designed to get you off the couch and get the blood flowing.

2. Get out of your comfort zones, and enjoy the adventure of serving alongside each other. As a couple, volunteer in your community. Serve together at church, sign up for a short-term mission trip, or volunteer at a local shelter.

3. Go to a professional or collegiate sporting event together. If you know nothing about the sport or the event, even better. Stretch yourself for the adventure, and try to find the lure behind the event.

4. Make a list of the five most popular local attractions in your area you have yet to visit. Then rank them in order of popularity or personal interest, and try to go to as many as time and money afford you. Make your list and ranking separate from your spouse's; then compare lists.

5. Go out on a date without spending more than ten dollars.

6. Save money and live your local dream date night. What restaurant would you most like to go to? What activity, show, or event would you like to attend yet never allow yourself to spend the money on? Pamper yourselves.

7. Choose a type of food you have never tried (e.g., Thai, Japanese, Indian, etc.), and go out to that restaurant together. Be risky with your choice on

the menu. Don't be afraid to try something new. Remember, it's about adventure.

8. Is there an activity, sport, or hobby neither one of you are that good at but would love to try together? Step out of your comfort zones and give it a try. You could go shooting at a gun range, ice-skating, kayaking, dancing, etc. Do something different than what you did on your laugh date.

9. Take a night and rearrange the furniture in your house. Go around and try new concepts and ideas for seeing your home differently. Leave it this way for a few weeks. If you don't like it, you can always change it back.

10. Dig out old family pictures and videos. Go through each of them, and reminisce on old adventures you had together or as a family. Use it as a catalyst to begin talking about and planning your next big adventure together.

ADVENTURE52

1. On a scale of 1 to 10, how adventurous is our life together?

2. Would you call me adventurous?

3. What was the last totally spontaneous thing we did together?

4. What do you think of when you hear the word *adventure*?

5. Do I have any adventures personally that you feel get in the way of us as a couple (e.g., hunting, shopping, golf, watching sports, etc.)?

6. As your spouse, how can I help you be more adventurous?

7. The biggest barrier to adventure in our marriage is _____.

8. Some creative ways to work around or overcome that barrier include _____.

9. When it comes to adventure in our marriage, I feel most loved when you _____.

10. Did you ever see your parents being adventurous?

11. Who in your life has shown you a great example of being adventurous?

12. When was the last time you felt really brave?

13. When was the last time you saw me do something courageous?

14. When was the last time we took a big risk as a couple?

15. What is your favorite action or adventure movie?

16. Before I turn _____ years old, I want to _____.

17. Have you ever done something you were really scared to do just to impress me?

18. When was the last time you felt genuinely scared?

19. What is your biggest fear?

20. Have you ever been in a situation where you wondered if you would actually survive?

21. When was the last time you felt truly alive?

22. If you could try at least one extreme sport, what would it be (e.g., skydiving, snowboarding, bungee jumping, scuba diving, etc.)?

23. What one outdoor activity would you like me to try?

24. The only thing keeping me from exercising more is _____.

25. Create a bucket list of five outdoor adventures we could accomplish together in the next year (e.g., horseback riding, four-wheeler riding, snowmobiling, waterskiing, etc.).

26. Create a bucket list of outdoor adventures we would like to try together in the next five years (e.g., skydiving, surfing, scuba diving, going on a safari, etc.).

27. What activity, sport, or hobby brings out a competitive, adventurous, tenacious spirit in each of us?

28. Create a bucket list of five of the world's most iconic places we would like to visit.

29. Where in the world are you most afraid to go?

30. Would you ever be willing to travel there? Why or why not?

31. If we sold all we owned and took off on an adventure for one year, where would we go and what would we do?

32. If we could save money and travel abroad, what one place would you like to visit? (Go ahead and start planning it!)

33. Is there a long weekend available for us to go on a road trip together?

34. If we could go away by car for a long weekend, where would we go? Where would we stay? What would we do?

35. If we could go away by plane for a long weekend, where would we go? Where would we stay? What would we do?

36. Would you be open to climbing a tree with me?

37. If someone told us we had an all-expenses-paid trip to the Amazon and only one hour to prepare for the trip, what would be your greatest roadblock to spontaneity? What could we do to overcome the roadblock?

38. If money were not an issue, what would your dream date night look like? What restaurant would you most like to go to? Activity?

39. Would our children say we are adventurous and spontaneous or timid and careful?

40. What if our next date was unplanned? We plan the date and time, but not the activity or duration. Does that sound fun or boring?

41. Think of a scene from one of your favorite movies and act it out together.

42. When was the last time we had a dance party together in our kitchen? Go for it!

43. When was the last time we chased each other around the house like a couple of kids?

44. Would you rather climb a mountain, kayak alongside whales, or bungee jump off a bridge? You must pick one.

45. What is your gut reaction when church leaders ask us to serve?

46. When was the last time you wanted to respond to a need in our church or community but delayed, procrastinated, or flat-out rejected it?

47. If I could serve anywhere in our church, I would serve _____.

48. I have never considered serving on a short-term trip to a foreign country because I feel _____.

49. If I had _____, I would give more at church.

50. Let's begin regularly praying for the following three ministries at our church:

_____

_____

_____

51. What is your greatest fear about getting more involved at church?

52. How would you feel if I committed more at church?

For more date night ideas, suggestions, and questions, please visit http://woodhills.org/datenightchallenge.

Chapter 6

The Annual Getaway

Come, my beloved, let us go to the countryside,
let us spend the night in the villages.

—Song of Songs 7:11

Amy and I have an ongoing debate as to which of our annual getaways was the best. It is a toss-up between an overnight in New York City and a weekend retreat in Colorado Springs. Both were special and definitely worth repeating.

In November 2011, we used airline miles and hotel points to take an overnight trip to New York City. Some people choose the beach. Others choose the mountains. My wife and I are new foodies and we like diversity in culture, so we chose the Big Apple.

A one night's stay was all the time we had, so we made the most of it. We flew out from Springfield, Missouri, at 6:00 a.m. and hit the ground at LaGuardia around 1:00 p.m. Then we took a forty-five-minute taxi ride to the Marriott Marquis in Times Square. It's a massive hotel on what feels like the busiest street in the world. We wasted no time checking in, dropping off our bags, and hitting the pavement.

We shopped, walked, and ate for the first five hours before taking in an 8:00 p.m. Broadway show. The tickets were a hundred dollars a pair from that last-minute ticket outlet on the north end of Times Square. About thirty minutes into the show, we realized that we had made a terrible mistake. The show was horribly vulgar. Listening to a ten-year-old kid repeatedly dropping the f-bomb wore me out. I looked over to Amy and said, "Let's not waste any more time." Her eyes lit up as if to say, "Great idea, our time is precious, and this is not the best use of it." Upon exiting, we walked around Times Square a bit before retiring to the room.

The room was the best part of the trip. *Bom-bom-chicky-chicky-bom-bom.* Hotel rooms on annual getaways provide the perfect environment for enjoying marital intimacy. First, they are kid-free. There is no chance of them waking in the night and coming into the room. You can sleep naked, like you used to do when you were first married. Our three family rules are not needed on these trips. The three rules are (1) pick your clothes up off the floor, (2) flush the toilet, (3) and don't bother Mom and Dad when they are wrestling.

Second, the room is clean, and you had nothing to do with cleaning it. It is luxurious, and you had nothing to do with furnishing it. Your shower has limitless hot water. You lounge around in three-hundred-dollar robes that you would never buy for home.

And don't forget about the ice bucket. Amy cracks up at me because I feel the need to have ice on hand even though I never use it. There's just something about having a bucket of ice by the bed that makes me feel rich. If you want to splurge on room service, great! We are usually quite full by the time we get back to the room, so food delivered to the room is not a temptation. If there's a minibar, go slow. I always find myself staring at the snacks and thinking, *There's no way I would sleep tonight if I ate this eight-dollar Snickers bar.*

However, we definitely splurged on room service during our second favorite annual getaway of all time in Colorado Springs. The Broadmoor is a one-of-a-kind hotel near the southern edge of the Rockies with a picturesque view of Pikes Peak. It is the perfect spot for any adventurer, but it's also great for anyone who enjoys five-star amenities. Again, it was an overnight getaway with the theme of food and love. We never left the room!

Upon check-in, we immediately slipped into our robes, jumped into bed, and perused the in-room dining menu. We ordered dinner and rested while we waited. About forty-five minutes later, we heard a knock at the door. That is always the signal for Amy to jump up and run into the bathroom. I tucked in my robe, tightened the belt, and answered the door.

The attendant wheeled in the cart and converted it into a round table with a white linen tablecloth. We even had fresh flowers as a centerpiece. I signed for the meal, the server departed, and Amy and I enjoyed one of the best meals of all time! We rarely eat while wearing nothing but robes, so this meal was extraspecial.

Sitting on the side of the table was a piece of cheesecake designed and plated by a sugar artist. It screamed, "Stop eating your vegetables and take me now!"

Amy spotted me eyeing the dessert. "Why don't we save that for later?" she said with a wink and a mischievous smile.

My heart raced as I said, "You mean to tell me that we get to enjoy this beautiful room, a four-fork dinner, make love, then eat some cheesecake? This is the perfect night!" And it was! Amy and I still refer to that night as "one of the best sex getaways of all time."

I hesitate sharing these getaways because I can already hear some readers thinking, *We don't have the money to take an annual getaway! This is only for an elite group.* As my son says, "You couldn't be more wronger!" Save your money. Stash some cash. Stay out of debt. Get creative. It is worth every penny.

Amy and I own a minivan with 120,000 miles and a Hyundai Sonata with 75,000 miles. They are paid off, and we have no debt. Whenever we consider buying a new car, we think about New York and Colorado and make the choice to prioritize our marriage above a new car. Vehicles may be your thing, and I won't judge you. For us, annual getaways are too important to jeopardize them with car payments.

I bet if Dave Ramsey or I spent some time with you, you would see that the money is there. It may take months to square away your budget; that is why I always budget with the end in mind. I want my marriage to be a priority in the home and that means the budget, too.

If you are in denial and refuse to find ways to prioritize and afford annual getaways, here are a few secrets for saving big:

1. Book your getaway in the off-season. Go to Phoenix or Palm Springs in the summer. Go to Branson, Missouri, in January and February. Avoid the big prices during peak season.

2. Use airline miles and hotel points. If your work does not involve travel, ask your family and friends to gift miles and points around the holidays and at birthdays.

3. Subscribe to travel websites. Look for the deals that include 80 to 90 percent off. Cruise ships are constantly advertising last-minute deals. Keep in mind, though, this requires major flexibility. You must be ready to go at a moment's notice. I have friends in Branson who schedule their vacation time every year with no definite plans. The time is blocked off, but they wait until just weeks before to plan where they are going. This will help the detailed among you learn spontaneity.

4. Combine business and pleasure. Bring your spouse on your next business trip and add a day. Amy and I are constantly coordinating overnight getaways with my speaking schedule. We know it raises our marital and sexual satisfaction, and *USA Today* recently validated our findings:

> A new survey out today by the U.S. Travel Association has found that couples who travel together have better relationships—and better sex—than those who don't.
>
> Nearly two-thirds of couples surveyed say a weekend getaway is more likely to spark romance in their relationship than a gift. Of the 1,100 U.S. adults surveyed, 72% think traveling inspires romance.
>
> More than three-quarters, or 77%, of those who travel as a couple say they have a good sex life, compared with 63% of couples who don't travel together. And 28% of the couples say their sex life actually improved after traveling together.

Of those couples, 40% say the improvement was permanent.[1]

On my speaking agreement with churches and organizations, I request travel for two. This allows me to bring Amy on a third or so of my trips. Most of the time, my whole family travels with me.

But if a speaking event places me in or near a romantic city, it's time for the kids to have a sleepover with Grandma and Grandpa. I'm taking Amy alone!

Annual getaways are vital for a hard break from the grind. Solomon and the Shulammite woman are a busy, hardworking couple. In Song of Songs 7, she invites Solomon on an out-of-town, overnight trip. This isn't any ordinary trip. This is an escape from the grind for the sole purpose of making love in the great outdoors:

> *Come, my beloved, let us go to the countryside,*
> *let us spend the night in the villages.*
> *Let us go early to the vineyards*
> *to see if the vines have budded,*
> *if their blossoms have opened,*
> *and if the pomegranates are in bloom—*
> *there I will give you my love.* (Song 7:11–12)

Their plan is to sleep in the villages. Sounds like a bed-and-breakfast if I've ever heard of one. Then they will get up early and head to the vineyards to make love. Whenever romance is building in the Song of Songs, it's always around the time of spring. Springtime is a great time for love.

Ladies, this is a powerful invitation to get your husband out of town. There are two ways to motivate your husband to take you on an annual getaway. The first way is to nag him. "We don't ever go anywhere." "We don't ever do anything." "We don't ever get away; it's never just us."

There is a better way, and it's the tactic of the Shulammite woman. "Honey, I would like to go away for a weekend and have sex." "We can get a room in a quaint hotel and enjoy unrushed, unhurried love outdoors, a lot of naked time outdoors." What a fantastic biblical invitation.

Like I said, years ago Amy and I bought a trampoline. When we assembled it, we thought the kids would get the most use out of it. Wrong!

In February 2012, a tornado hit our town and ripped through our backyard around 2:00 a.m. Our back-door neighbors lost their roofs. We lost our backyard furniture, playground, and, yes, our trampoline.

Around 7:00 a.m., I heard my son screaming from the back door. I raced to see what was the matter.

My son yelled, "Dad, oh no! Look what happened to the trampoline!" It was upside down in the cedar trees, torn to shreds.

I looked at the trampoline, then looked at him and cried, "I knooooow! That will be the first thing we replace, Son!"

(I feel I would not be a good pastor if I neglected to give you this warning. If you decide to make love outdoors, be sure it is at night. I don't need readers getting arrested and blaming me.)

Can an Annual Getaway Restore Our Marriage?

Our church is so committed to the idea of an annual getaway, we host an event every year in Branson called Love and Laughter. We theme it each year to keep it new and fresh. In 2012, we hosted Love, Laughter and Country Music. In 2013, we switched it up a bit with Love, Laughter and Rock and Roll. In 2014, we'll schedule Love, Laughter and a Culinary Experience.

Each January, we take over the Chateau on the Lake resort and invite couples from all over the country to a great time of loving and laughing. Last year, we had fifteen states represented and sold out the resort.

At each event we invite my buddy Paul Harris, a local comedian here in Branson. He's a cross between Larry the Cable Guy and a *Hee Haw* regular. Very funny. My buddies Gary Smalley and Joe White join me in talking about marriage. Most of all, we spend time enjoying the amenities of the hotel, like the spa, theater, library lounge, pool, and atrium. The goal of this getaway is to stay far away from anything that would resemble a husband-bashing seminar or a "Woman, give your husband more sex" conference. We want the entire weekend to reflect Ecclesiastes 9:9, enjoying life together.

We are amazed each year by the turnout and impact of this annual getaway. Story after story gets back to us about how it radically changed couples. Seriously? A weekend of laughter, fun, and play can help transform a couple's marriage? Yep! We know that Christ is the only one who brings change to the human heart. So why does a weekend getaway facilitate such life change?

For the same reason couples experience miracles at the National Institute of Marriage—time away from the grind allows room in our lives for God to work. Pastor Bill Hybels is known for saying, "Don't allow your work for God to destroy God's work in you." For some of us, the pace of our lives leaves God no room to shake us up. A weekend getaway slows us down and opens our hearts to miraculous life change.

Do you know who needs this event the most? Parents! Mom and Dad forget how to enjoy life and each other. All types of parents show up. From parents of toddlers to parents of college students (i.e., empty nesters), they all come back year after year to prioritize laughter, fun, and play.

Tim and Lisa from St. Louis are huge fans of this getaway. Married for twenty years, they are empty nesters. By their own admission, they had nothing left for each other once the kids left home. They stopped enjoying each other fifteen or so years ago. In December 2007, they were done. The kids were out of the house, and either Tim or Lisa would soon be gone too. They fell into the pattern we see in so many boomer couples. They worked so hard to raise kids that they forgot how to enjoy each other. There was nothing left of their marriage.

I met Tim and Lisa on a Sunday morning in August 2009. They were a happy couple with smiles from ear to ear.

"You both sure look happy," I said as I introduced myself.

"Life is great," Tim said. "You don't have a clue who we are, do you?"

"I'm sorry," I said with a deer-in-the-headlights look. "Where are you from?"

"We're from St. Louis, and we are here today because you are renewing our vows at the end of the second service," Tim said.

It all came back to me. My assistant had this on my calendar. "Fantastic. I'm looking forward to it," I said. What they said next floored me.

"Ted, the Love and Laughter Getaway saved our marriage!" Lisa said through tears.

You've got to be kidding me! Tim and Lisa attended our first ever Love and Laughter. The event was a whirlwind filled with nonstop laughter. I know content is important at any marriage event, but this event leans on delivery.

"That weekend changed everything for us. We remembered laughing together years earlier and had no idea why or when the laughter ever left our home," Lisa said.

Tim and Lisa sat through both services at Woodland Hills that morning. When the auditorium cleared out after the second service, our worship pastor played a little tinkly music and invited Tim and Lisa to step up onstage. They renewed their vows right on the spot. They held hands as they faced each other and through many tears apologized for letting their marriage slip away. They recommitted to a lifetime of serving and enjoying one another. Our softy worship pastor was choking back tears. They read and prayed that God would renew a bond that was lost to their kid-centered home.

We invite you to Branson sometime to experience Love and Laughter. If you can't make it, no problem. Here are a few spots around the country that Amy and I visit on our annual getaways. All of these spots are great fun for couples and families.

Sanibel Island: Located west of Fort Myers, Florida, Sanibel beaches offer some of the best shelling in the country. We fill bags with shells and enjoy the diner-style food offered around the island.

Paradise Point (San Diego, California): We love staying on the bay side of this resort. I use one of the small crabs crawling on the beach as bait, and the last time we were there I caught a three-pound sea bass. Enjoy a campfire and s'mores on the beach.

Marys Lake Lodge and Resort (Estes Park, Colorado): We love horseback riding through Rocky Mountain National Park and waking up each morning to moose and elk right outside our door.

JW Marriott Scottsdale Camelback Inn Resort & Spa (Scottsdale, Arizona): The on-site restaurant is one of our favorites in the country. There is a hiking trail through the desert landscape, and the pools are heated. Our family loves this resort.

The King and Prince Beach & Golf Resort (St. Simons Island, Georgia): This was our first real annual getaway as a couple. We had little money, but again, booking in the off-season saved us a ton. We spent one night here, then moved over to the Hampton Inn for night two. We spent the weekend fishing from the pier. We brought home a hundred blue crab, boiled them, cleaned them, and had enough meat to make about four crab cakes. We haven't made crab cakes since.

Asheville, North Carolina: We stayed in an economy hotel but spent the day touring the Biltmore estate. The Biltmore mansion was built by George Washington Vanderbilt between 1888 and 1902 and is one of the largest privately owned houses in the United States. Including nearly seven thousand acres of land, the estate is made up of 250 buildings and structures. [2]

Savannah, Georgia: It doesn't matter where we sleep; I love this town. You shop a little in historic downtown, followed by lunch at Paula Deen's Lady & Sons, and conclude the day with a walk on the beach on Tybee Island.

The Magnificent Mile (Chicago, Illinois): This is a fun, fast, big-city getaway. There are smoking-hot deals on hotels, too. Great food and great shopping.

The FLY Journal (#funlovingyou)

Plan your annual getaway. (This might be a great activity to do during your dream date night!)

Date:
Child care:
Budget (fill in all that apply):

Flights:
Hotel:
Parking:
Meals:
Car rental:

Gas:

Tolls:

Baggage fees:

Shows/Entertainment:

Other:

Flight/Driving information:

Directions to hotel:

Restaurant reservations:

Chapter 7

Enjoying Marriage More Than the Wedding

Come out, and look, you daughters of Zion. Look on King Solomon wearing a crown, the crown with which his mother crowned him on the day of his wedding, the day his heart rejoiced.

—Song of Songs 3:11

Second only to your salvation, your wedding day is the greatest day of your life. Your salvation committed you to Christ. Your wedding committed you to your spouse.

Many couples put time, money, and energy into the planning and execution of their weddings to create unforgettable memories. The same is true for marriage. With plenty of thought, investment, and hard work, the celebration continues from the wedding into a lifetime of enjoying marriage.

I love everything about weddings. The festive and joyous atmosphere grabs me from the moment I walk into the rehearsal and lingers for days afterward. It is intoxicating. My passion in life and ministry is showing couples how that joy and festivity are more than possible long after the cake is cut.

My family and I recently traveled to Carrefour, Haiti, to dedicate a school. Woodland Hills Family Church helped rebuild the school, which was destroyed by the 2010 earthquake. We traveled there the day after Christmas 2012 and made it in time to attend a Haitian wedding. Our whole family could not wait to celebrate marriage in a foreign country. Little did we know that the Haitian people love long weddings. Dare I say, *epic* weddings!

The wedding started at 4:00 p.m. inside the school's cafeteria. It was 97 degrees outside and about 110 degrees inside the non-air-conditioned building. They reserved the front row for the Cunninghams. We had no idea that we were the guests of honor. We had front-row seats and participated in everything. Observing was not an option.

The processional was a beautiful dance by the wedding party that lasted about forty-five minutes. There were four chairs up front for the bride, groom, and bride's parents. The groom sat with the bride's mother in two chairs behind dad and daughter. The giving of the bride took about one hour. The groom was giddy, but everyone else was stoic.

About an hour and forty-five minutes in, I looked over at my son and saw that he was wiped out. His cheeks were red. His hair was soaked with sweat. Our seven-year-old was a champ; he didn't complain but gently turned to me and whispered, "This is the longest wedding ever!"

Pastor Ficque invited me up to say a special blessing over the couple. The interpreter delivered my blessing in French. I returned to my seat, thinking the wedding was over. I was wrong.

After two and half hours, the pastor came over to me and said, "Your family looks tired and hot, and I want to give you the opportunity to step out and go back to your hotel before we start the preaching portion of the ceremony."

Our family collectively raised our eyebrows as if to say, "*What?*" There were four preachers in attendance, not including me, and they each had a turn to deliver a sermon. We graciously accepted his invitation to be dismissed. Later we learned that the ceremony went on for another few hours. If we stayed, I would have lost another two pounds.

In Solomon's and Jesus's days, weddings were long too. They lasted for days. The celebration would begin with the exchange of vows and entering into a covenant relationship. Shortly thereafter, they would consummate the marriage before continuing to party.

In John 2 we read that Jesus was an invited guest at a wedding. This is where He performed His first miraculous sign:

> On the third day a wedding took place at Cana in Galilee. Jesus' mother was there, and Jesus and his disciples had also been invited to the wedding. When the wine was gone, Jesus' mother said to him, "They have no more wine." (vv. 1–3)

I absolutely love the fact that Jesus's mother pointed out to her son the need for more wine. In other words, "Son, do Your thing." No wine meant that the wedding celebration was over. Jesus honored His mother by creating more wine. When this text is preached, we tend to focus on the miracle. I love how Jesus kept the party going. His gift to the wedding was an extended time of celebration. I know too many preachers who preach this text according to church traditions rather than within the biblical and historical context. What a shame. That approach blows right past the gift Jesus offered the bride and groom.

As we return to the Song of Songs chapter 3, Solomon's duet with the Shulammite woman builds to a climax with the anticipation of a wedding. It may be the shortest chapter in the book, but it is a defining moment. Solomon describes a wedding with traditions unfamiliar to us, yet we still observe these core elements in our ceremonies some three thousand years later:

> *All night long on my bed*
> > *I looked for the one my heart loves;*
> > *I looked for him but did not find him.*
> *I will get up now and go about the city,*
> > *through its streets and squares;*
> *I will search for the one my heart loves.*
> > *So I looked for him but did not find him.*
> *The watchmen found me*
> > *as they made their rounds in the city.*
> > *"Have you seen the one my heart loves?"*
> *Scarcely had I passed them*
> > *when I found the one my heart loves.*
> *I held him and would not let him go*
> > *till I had brought him to my mother's house,*

to the room of the one who conceived me.
Daughters of Jerusalem, I charge you
    by the gazelles and by the does of the field:
Do not arouse or awaken love
    until it so desires.
Who is this coming up from the wildnerness
    like a column of smoke,
perfumed with myrrh and incense
    made from all the spices of the merchant?
Look! It is Solomon's carriage,
    escorted by sixty warriors,
    the noblest of Israel,
all of them wearing the sword,
    all experienced in battle,
each with his sword at his side,
    prepared for the terrors of the night.
King Solomon made for himself the carriage;
    he made it of wood from Lebanon.
Its posts he made of silver,
    its base of gold.
Its seat was upholstered with purple,
    its interior inlaid with love.
Daughters of Jerusalem, come out,
    and look, you daughters of Zion.
Look on King Solomon wearing a crown,
    the crown with which his mother crowned him
on the day of his wedding,
    the day his heart rejoiced. (Song 3:1–11)

The Shulammite woman is now a bride. The chapter begins with a dream of her union with the shepherd-king, Solomon. Her desire and passion for the exclusivity of marriage wakes her up at night. For the last time while courting, she reminds the daughters of Jerusalem to "not arouse or awaken love until it so desires" (v. 5). The time is here for her all-consuming love to be fully realized. The wedding is here, and the marriage begins.

Their wedding was three thousand years ago. One would think that there are few similarities between their wedding and ours. However, the traditions of their wedding endure to this day.

There was a processional (v. 6). They had a wedding party (vv. 7–8). The preparations took time, money, and hard work (vv. 9–10). Solomon's mom blessed the union (v. 11). Sound familiar? Amy and I had a similar wedding. We had fifteen in our weddings party, not sixty. We had a processional, although I was not carried in on a couch like Solomon. We drove off in an Enterprise rental car, not a homemade carriage. We spent five months preparing for our wedding. Amy's parents and mine were there to give their blessings. Our wedding, like yours, was the defining moment that committed Amy and me to exclusivity in marriage.

Planning, Hard Work, and Location, Location, Location

I love destination weddings, beach weddings, family-backyard weddings, after-Sunday-morning-service weddings, casual weddings, theme weddings, and, dare I say it, *elopement*. I've officiated weddings ranging in cost from a few hundred dollars all the way up to the six-figure mark. I've performed ceremonies under large tents, in gardens, on rocky bluffs, and in castles, chapels, and churches. I've stood before intimate gatherings of twenty guests and sprawling events for five hundred. It really doesn't matter the size or budget; all weddings require planning.

Planning a wedding can be hard work. Even if you plan a small wedding or elopement, your to-do list can be several pages long.

Most brides I meet with enjoy the planning. I rarely hear "I'm sick of this wedding" or "I just want to get the wedding over with." What I do hear is "We are having so much fun planning." "This Saturday me and the girls are starting with brunch, then trying on dresses." "We are going to a tasting later today." "We have pre-marital counseling with our pastor later on this week." Early on, couples tackle wedding planning with great enthusiasm. Closer to the wedding, enthusiasm and exhaustion walk down the aisle hand in hand.

It strikes me that the work required to pull off a one-day wedding is celebrated as a dream come true, while the work required to make a marriage thrive is belittled as exhausting and hardly worth it. If we work hard to plan a fairy-tale wedding, why can't we work just as hard to plan a fairy-tale marriage?

Amy and I want Corynn to get married at Disney World. We dream about one day waking up to a Disneyparks.com offer of 90 percent off Disney destination weddings. If that day comes, we're in!

The wedding my wife and I keep talking about took place at our favorite resort in southwest Missouri. Johnny Morris, the founder of Bass Pro Shops, built Big Cedar. Now before you guess that our favorite wedding included a bunch of rednecks at a marina with strings of shotgun-shell lights, you need to know that Big Cedar is a luxurious resort and spa in a woodland setting. It's the wedding we've dreamed about for our daughter, if she declines Disney.

The wedding ceremony took place at sunset. The bride and groom hailed from opposite ends of the country and traveled to Branson with only their immediate families. Big Cedar sits on Table Rock Lake with several dozen cabins and lodges lining the shore. This particular wedding took place on a point with a 180-degree view of the water. It was gorgeous.

Amy and I walked into this quaint cabin and were greeted by twenty to thirty people laughing and having a good time. We mingled for thirty minutes or so before I accompanied the bride and groom out onto the balcony just before sunset. I stood with my back up against the balcony. The bride and groom faced each other, holding hands, and the best man and maid of honor stood by their sides. And through the double doors stood their family and my precious bride, Amy. The sunset painted our backdrop. They exchanged vows and rings and stepped inside for a few photos, cake, and punch. It was relaxed, picturesque, tear filled, and over-the-top memorable.

Amy and I have big plans for our twenty-fifth wedding anniversary. Our wedding was memorable, but on the cheaper side. She still has regrets over our choice in photographer and wedding cake. Our discontentment with our own wedding cake grew after watching *Cake Boss* and *Food Network Challenge*. Now that we have a few more bucks, I'm planning a special destination vow renewal in eight years. Who knows, we may take that Disney deal for ourselves.

The Parents

Mom and dad play a very significant role in the wedding. I know what you are thinking: *Yeah, the bride's parents pay.* More than financial commitment, they have two primary responsibilities: they bless the union and "cut the strings." Solomon wore the crown "with which his mother crowned him on the day of his wedding" (3:11) to signify her blessing and approval of the union. This is gut-wrenching for parents, and it is for that reason that I believe this should be the slowest part of the wedding.

I tell the dad prior to every ceremony, "When I ask who gives this woman to be married to this man, you respond with, 'Her mother and I.' Then I want you to turn and give your daughter a blessing. Take your time. No rush. The words you speak to her at that moment she will never forget."

I've yet to watch a dad hold it together at that point in the service. They lose it every time. As a dad, I get it. She is leaving my home, protection, to be joined to this punk. Sorry, that last part just popped out. I apologize … sort of.

My daughter, Corynn, is convinced that she's never leaving home. At seven, she's made up her mind that Mom and Dad take such great care of her that she'll just stay.

But she knows I'll have none of that.

One of the hardest questions Corynn has ever asked me is, "Dad, who do you love more, me or Mom?"

Ouch! Naturally my first response to a question like that is to act like I didn't hear the question, or I squint my eyes as though I didn't understand the question. She has me wrapped around her little finger.

"I love your mommy and you both," I say gently, "but God wants me to love Mommy in a different way. Your mommy and I are together for life in a covenant relationship. We will be together until one of us goes to heaven or Jesus returns. But you, Corynn, will not be with us forever. You will one day leave our home and start a family of your own."

Corynn is quick to reply, "I want to be with you and Mommy forever."

"You can't be with us forever, Corynn," I say.

As tears form in her eyes, she glares at me and says, "I am going to college online and staying home forever. You can't make me leave." While I must admit I like the sound of that from a tuition stand-point, I want her to know that separation from Mom and Dad is actually a sign of health and maturity. She will need to leave home one day.

There's a very important verse in the Bible that speaks to parent-ing in preparation for marriage: "That is why a man leaves his father and mother and is united to his wife, and they become one flesh" (Gen. 2:24). The King James Version uses the word *cleave* to convey being united. In other words, the bond between husband and wife is to be stronger than the bond between parent and child.

Marriage involves a new priority relationship. When you see the word *leaves*, you may think you need to move a thousand miles away from mom and dad. However, the focus of this text is not *geographical*. Most young couples actually live in close proximity to their parents and move away later. The focus of this text is *relational*.

"Leaving" is the idea that no relationship, apart from your relationship with God, is more important than your marriage. To leave means to forsake, depart from, leave behind, and abandon. Say good-bye to Mom and Dad.

From the time God spoke Genesis 2:24 and through the first several thousand years of human history, kids grew up, became adults, and left home. Starting marriage well requires leaving home. Cut the strings. Love and honor your parents, but call home less, buy your own clothes, work out conflict in your marriage without your parents meddling, seek the input of your spouse over your parents, and never, ever compare your spouse to a parent.

I love when a mom approaches me during her child's wedding and says, "I don't feel like I am losing a son today, but like I am gaining a daughter."

I usually respond with, "Nope, you are losing a son."

Do you want to enjoy your marriage? Then cut the strings. This process should start before the wedding, but if not, a wedding is a grand ceremony to officially change the relationship.

One of my most awkward moments was at a wedding rehearsal when a dad refused to give his daughter away. When I asked, "Who gives this woman to be married to this man?" Dad was silent. As my son, Carson, says, looking over his glasses and out of the corner of his mouth, "Awkwaaaaard!"

I repeated the question. Still nothing. When I probed the dad, he said, "I will not give my daughter away, but I will be happy to share her."

"Oops," I said as I turned toward the groom. "Looks like we won't be having a wedding tomorrow."

Dad was strong, but with pressure from Mom and the gathered guests, he caved. We had a wedding the next day. Through tears he said, "Her mother and I."

Wedding Party, Family, and Friends

Months before your special day, you sent out invitations to aunts, uncles, cousins, coworkers, college buddies, and childhood friends. You decided who would stand beside you and worked down the line from there.

I love joking with ushers at weddings, "So, you must be cousins. You are close to the groom, just not that close." Picking a best man and maid of honor is a hard choice for some couples. *Will I hurt the feelings of those not picked? If he ends up as an usher, what does that say? Who do I declare as my closest friend?* That decision makes a bold statement to everyone.

The wedding party is one element of modern weddings that has lost significant meaning. Solomon was "escorted by sixty warriors, the noblest of Israel, all of them wearing the sword, all experienced in battle, each with his sword at his side, prepared for the terrors of the night" (Song 3:7–8). His wedding party had a purpose: to keep Solomon safe and secure. No one or no thing would disrupt this holy union.

Our wedding parties are chosen for social purposes rather than protection. We want our friends gathered around to join with us in the celebration. When I officiate a wedding, I add the element of accountability and protection. Because I believe "marriage should be honored by all" (Heb. 13:4), I encourage every person in attendance to become a marriage advocate, starting with the wedding party and working toward family and friends. It comes out in my welcome:

> Family and friends, we are gathered here today in
> the sight of God and man to witness the marriage

of Rick Seger and Tricia Sedlacek. Marriage, which is ordained by God, is an act whereby two people become one. These two lives will today join together in a covenant relationship.

You are here for a purpose today. As a witness you are here to observe the commitment made here between Rick and Tricia. As family and friends, you may be called upon to remind them of these vows. Be an advocate for their marriage. Hope in their marriage. Speak words of blessing over their marriage. Pray for their marriage. Hold them accountable to the commitment they make this day.

As Rick and Tricia begin their new life together, we trust and know that God, who has brought them to this point, will continue to nurture and bless their marriage. This holy estate of matrimony is sacred. It is a relationship of giving, not taking, sharing, not withholding.

Starting today, Rick and Tricia will become a part of one another. Not only will they share the same home, but their hearts will be linked together with the love of the Lord Jesus Christ.

So today, Rick and Tricia, we rejoice with you. You are surrounded by loving family and caring friends who have great hope for your future.

I tear up reading those words. Please, please, please do not shy away from leaning into family and friends for support long after the wedding is over. In chapter 2, we discussed symptom 6 of a stuck marriage: when your marriage gets stuck in the grind, you isolate yourself from others. Instead, press into biblical community, and be reminded of the vows you exchanged.

Also, be a marriage advocate to the marriages around you. It is not a job solely reserved for pastors and clergy. You can challenge family and friends to work at enjoying marriage. Be a marriage warrior equipped for battle. You don't need to bring a weapon to your next wedding, but bring the protection and accountability.

The Pastor and the Message

If I could, I would do weddings full-time. I hate when my schedule keeps me from doing a wedding. Could anything be better for a preacher? I get to speak on my passion and share the gospel with a captive audience. The message directed at the bride and groom always hits the couple who is struggling and considering divorce.

My family often attends with me. We all get to enjoy a pricey meal for free, and to top it all off, there's the icing on the cake. Weddings are the only time you get to enjoy that special buttercream frosting. They should call it "weddingcream" frosting.

The pastor part of the wedding is quickly being replaced too. Just like shorter, streamlined ceremonies, some couples choose a justice of the peace over a pastor. Let me make the case for a wedding with a pastor.

The prophet Malachi linked character to commitment when he said, "The LORD is the witness between you and the wife of your youth. You have been unfaithful to her, though she is your partner, the wife of your marriage covenant" (Mal. 2:14).

Many couples want to hire a pastor to serve as a justice of the peace rather than to hold a ceremony where the Lord serves as both witness and judge of character. Past generations asked the church and pastor for a blessing over their union. The potential couple would go to the church and submit themselves to the spiritual authority there to receive a blessing to marry.

Nowadays couples ask pastors and elders to validate their spouse selection. Usually they want a church wedding but not necessarily a church marriage. At Woodland Hills, when one of the pastors begins to explain what a church wedding entails, many couples seek out a pastor from another church. That is why one of our initial questions in premarital counseling is, "How much do you want the church and the community at Woodland Hills Family Church to be involved in holding you accountable to your vows long after your wedding?"

I beg you, if you haven't already, plug into a solid local church on the day you return from your honeymoon. Join a small group or Sunday school class where you can be in fellowship with other believers. Give those in the biblical community the freedom to speak into your lives. Your marriage is counting on it. Submit to the leaders of your church, and respect their authority. Don't bolt when they say or do something you don't like. You need them to point out sin in your life. Sometimes they will need to point out sin that is obvious. Other times they will need to point out sin that is leading you down an even more destructive path: "The sins of some are obvious, reaching the place of judgment ahead of them; the sins of others trail behind them" (1 Tim. 5:24).

When your sin is blatant and flagrant, good leaders will call you on it. We all need accountability, and the church is there to help us be men and women of God. Follow their leadership by obeying: "Obey your leaders and submit to them, for they keep watch over your souls as those who will give an account. Let them do this with joy and not with grief, for this would be unprofitable for you" (Heb. 13:17 NASB).

A church wedding is only the start; it's even better to have a church marriage. For almost seventeen years now, Amy and I have been leaning on the support of our church family, especially the older men and women in our congregation. Don't be afraid to ask for help when you need it.

Good pastoral counseling reminds you of your vows. The vows and the exchange of rings go hand in hand at the ceremonies I officiate:

> Do you, Tricia, take Rick to be your husband to love and cherish, honor and respect, in sickness and in health, for richer or for poorer, in good times and in bad, focusing on meeting his needs, rather than just meeting your own?
>
> *"I do!"*
>
> Do you, Rick, take Tricia to be your wife to love and cherish, honor and respect, in sickness and in health, for richer or for poorer, in good times and in bad, focusing on meeting her needs, rather than just meeting your own?
>
> *"I do!"*
>
> May we now have the rings?
>
> These rings have no beginning and no end. They represent the nature of agape love. Love that is

self-sacrificing. They will represent the love and trust that Rick and Tricia promise to each other this day.

Rick, will you take this ring and place it upon Tricia's finger, and as you do, repeat to her, after me, these words:

I give you this ring as a token of my love and commitment to live with you in marriage from this day forward. In the name of the Father, Son, and Holy Spirit.

Tricia, will you take this ring and place it upon Rick's finger, and as you do, repeat to him, after me, these words:

I give you this ring as a token of my love and commitment to live with you in marriage from this day forward. In the name of the Father, Son, and Holy Spirit.

These vows and the exchange of rings lead right into the unity candle. Less than half of the couples I marry desire to use a unity candle. I can be quite persuasive, though, and nine out of ten of those couples end up using one. The unity candle is my second, much shorter sermon:

With the unity candle lit, we pray and make the grand pronouncement of marriage.

Inasmuch as Rick and Tricia have exchanged vows and rings, before God and the gathered witnesses, by virtue of the authority entrusted to me as a minister of Jesus Christ, and in agreement with

the laws of the state of Missouri, I now pronounce
them husband and wife.

Earlier in the ceremony I prepare the wedding guests for this
pronouncement. I tell them that there will be three places at the very
end of the ceremony where they will hoot, holler, scream, clap, and
stomp their feet as though their favorite team has just won the Super
Bowl or World Series. We even take a moment to practice until we
reach the desired decibel level.

Once the official pronouncement is made, the place goes bal-
listic! Deafening cheers fill the place for what seems like forever. That
is one of three cheers.

"What God has joined together, let no man separate. Rick, you
may kiss the bride," I declare. For the second time, the gathered witnesses erupt with screams and applause.

As the applause sustains, the bride and groom turn and face
the congregation. I step to the left, place my hand on the groom's
shoulder, and say, "It is an honor for me to be the first to introduce
to you Mr. and Mrs. Rick Seger!" The upbeat music fills the place,
friends and family cheer, and the Segers head down the aisle with a
skip in their step.

And all God's people say, "Amen!" Now you see why I love weddings! And the reception is still to come.

Food, Wine, and Dancing

I have never been drunk a day in my life. I do not know what
it feels like to have a hangover. Growing up, I never once saw

my parents even sip alcohol. Our church and pastor taught total abstinence.

I took my first sip of wine three years ago. I drank twice before then, but I do not count either time. My first accidental drink was at a wedding when I was twenty. I drank from the wrong punch bowl. My second accidental drink was the year after Amy and I married while we were on a trip from Georgia to Texas to visit Dallas Theological Seminary. Hello! We stopped at a gas station in Louisiana. While the gas was pumping, I bought a cherry Slurpee for Amy and a lime Slurpee for me. We were ten miles down the road before Amy discovered that she had a strawberry daiquiri and I had a margarita. Close call.

My wife and I enjoy wine paired with great food. We drink occasionally with no desire or temptation to ever get drunk.

Food and wine are great gifts from our Lord. When we stop viewing them as gifts, we misuse them. Eating too much food is gluttony. Drinking too much wine is drunkenness. Both are sins. The overconsumption is the sin, not the food and wine themselves.

The first miraculous sign Jesus performed was at a wedding. Since weddings in His day lasted for days, providing food and drink for that long of a party was costly. I love this story of celebration, wine, and salvation:

> When the wine was gone, Jesus' mother said to him, "They have no more wine."
>
> "Woman, why do you involve me?" Jesus replied. "My hour has not yet come."

His mother said to the servants, "Do whatever he tells you."

Nearby stood six stone water jars, the kind used by the Jews for ceremonial washing, each holding from twenty to thirty gallons.

Jesus said to the servants, "Fill the jars with water"; so they filled them to the brim.

Then he told them, "Now draw some out and take it to the master of the banquet."

They did so, and the master of the banquet tasted the water that had been turned into wine. He did not realize where it had come from, though the servants who had drawn the water knew. Then he called the bridegroom aside and said, "Everyone brings out the choice wine first and then the cheaper wine after the guests have had too much to drink; but you have saved the best till now."

What Jesus did here in Cana of Galilee was the first of the signs through which he revealed his glory; and his disciples believed in him. (John 2:3–11)

If we take the low figure, Jesus created 120 gallons of wine. This was not cheap wine. The master of the banquet called it the best wine. In today's measurements, Jesus produced over six hundred bottles of wine. If it were a Kendall-Jackson pinot noir, that's about $12,000 in wine. But it was the "best," so I must assume it was a lot more than that. What a great gift for the wedding party!

Amy and I enjoy long meals. Our longest meal to date was four and a half hours on New Year's Eve 2012. We took our time working through seven courses with our good friends David and Jill Jones at Table 22 in Branson, Missouri. Months later, we still talk about the fun and fellowship of that night.

You don't need a special occasion as big as a wedding to enjoy a great meal together. Make it simple or fancy, cheap or expensive, red or white. It can be as simple as opening one bottle of wine and pairing it with a couple of pieces of cheese. You may want to go a little fancier. Cook a gourmet meal together, and make it about small portions and presentation. Most at-home meals are fast, large portions. Plan a four-course meal and prepare it together. Spend a day or two at the beginning of the week planning this meal, take another day to shop together for it, and at the end of the week prepare the meal together. Think fresh. Get fresh fish, or buy your bread from a bakery. Get the makings for a salad from an open-air market. Cook, plate, and even drizzle the sauce. Put some love into the meal.

How about the music? The Cunningham home is full of music and laughter. Our kids regularly plug the iPod into the speaker system and get their dance on for us after dinner. Try it. One fun idea is to create your wedding playlist. Whether your wedding music was on vinyl, 8-track, cassette, or compact disc, it is time to create a playlist.

Don't forget about the pictures. Every wedding has a photographer. Weddings create memories worth capturing. It starts with the formal pictures at the ceremony but quickly turns fun with the smashing of the cake in the face, the throwing of the bouquet, and the first dance. Pull out your wedding pictures regularly, and share them with your kids, family, and friends. Display your pictures in a prominent place in your home.

Reminiscing about your wedding is a great way to celebrate your marriage. What did you love? What would you change? Who brought the most laughs? What wedding gifts do you still use today? Remember family members who were there and have since passed away.

There is one more thing you can do to enjoy your marriage more than the wedding: plan another wedding. The official term is *vow renewal*. These are the best!

In February 2013 during a Twoignite Marriage Sunday, our church invited couples to the altar to renew their vows. The band played as forty-eight couples walked the aisle. That service went down in the books as one of the top five weekends at Woodland Hills.

Of the forty-eight couples who renewed, the best line I heard that morning was, "Ted, we were not Christians when we got married. This morning was so special now that we understand what a biblical marriage is all about."

Couples renew vows for different reasons. First, the most common vow renewal is to celebrate an anniversary. Guys, the best way to do this is to surprise your wife. It's an added bonus if you write your own vows.

Second, some couples plan a special service after a tough or dry season in their marriage. I rarely find myself in the position to advocate for divorce, but I do regularly help couples separate. A strategic separation is a better alternative to divorce. Please don't hear me saying that I work to separate couples. Not at all. This is a rare occurrence but extremely effective in saving marriages. I advocate for this only when I meet with a couple who tells me, "We filed the papers already." "I am dating someone new." "I don't feel safe." "It's over." "We've tried everything." "I have no more energy to continue, so this is it." In such cases, drastic measures are required.

A separation gives both husband and wife time for God to work. The guidelines are strict. No dating other people while you are married. I know that sounds absurd, but it is more common than you might think. You are allowed to date only each other during this separation. We need a plan. I like to set a date for a vow-renewal ceremony within six months so we have something to work toward. In that time I regularly meet with the couple to help them learn how to date and communicate. Some of the best vow renewals are from couples who commit to enjoying a marriage they never dreamed possible.

Third, I love the couples who want to renew their commitment because they now understand the true meaning of marriage, rooted in the Lord Jesus Christ. Their desire is for the Lord to bless the marriage.

At all weddings and vow renewals, I love asking family and friends to gather around the couple and lay hands on them and pray. This meaningful touch and spoken blessing stays with the couple. Again, this is a moment we do not want to rush.

Whether or not you plan to renew your vows officially, spend time rewriting your promises to each other now. With the life and parenting experience you've gained since you became husband and wife, what would you include in your updated vows? What do you love about your mate even more now than when you said, "I do"?

Read your renewed promises to each other, and put them where you'll be reminded of the love and life you share.

Amy and I, under the leadership and mentoring of Dr. Gary Smalley, took the time years ago to rewrite our vows and added many new promises.

The Cunningham Marriage Constitution (Perfect for Vow Renewals)

Preamble: When we wed, I committed to love and cherish you all the days of my life, and I affirm that commitment today. I love you dearly. My goal is to create in our marriage a place of security in which you and I can share everything in safety and honor without fear and grow together in deeper love and intimacy. To confirm my commitment to this goal, I willingly make these five solemn promises to you.

I promise to gain control of my emotions by continually examining my deepest beliefs and striving to make them consistent with what God's Word says. I take sole responsibility for my beliefs with the understanding that they, not you, determine my emotions, words, thoughts, and actions. Thus I lift from you the burden of being responsible for any of my ultimate life quality. In essence, you are fired as my source of life.

I promise to be filled by God. God is my source of joy and love. My love for you will be His love flowing through me. I will receive your love as overflow from Him. I will base the security of our marriage on making Christ my boss. I will strive to conform to His image and follow all His commands (Eph. 5:25–26; Phil. 4:19).

I promise to find God's best in every trial. I give you the security of knowing that the negative things that happen in our marriage will not destroy my love for you. I will not expect perfection from you but will use even the irritations between us as opportunities to see my blind spots and foster my personal growth. I will call on the power of Christ to root out my weaknesses (Rom. 8:28; James 1:12; Rom. 5:3–5).

I promise to listen and communicate with love. I will value every word you speak as a window to your heart. I will honor your opinions, feelings, needs, and beliefs so that you will feel free to speak honestly and openly with full security in my love for you. I will be open with you in communicating my heart and will consider your feelings and needs in all my words. I will help you solve every disagreement with me until you feel like a winner (Eph. 4:29).

I promise to serve you all the days of my life. I will fight all tendencies toward selfishness in me and focus on keeping you, your needs, and your goals before me at all times. I will continue to hide God's most important words in my heart, serving you willingly and wholeheartedly, just as Christ served His disciples not only in small, humble ways but also by giving His life for them and for us as well (Gal. 5:13).

Signature _____ Date _____

Signature _____ Date _____

The FLY Journal (#funlovingyou)

Does our marriage get the same amount of investment and planning as our wedding did?

Are we submitted to biblical authority and accountability?

Are we plugged into biblical community?

Are we committed to our vows?

Is our marriage a celebration of what God is doing in our life together?

Does our marriage model the gospel of Jesus Christ?

Chapter 8

The Fun (and Safe) Bedroom

Eat, friends, and drink; drink your fill of love.
—Song of Songs 5:1

A few years back I challenged the couples in our church to get a little frisky. I encouraged each wife to go home and throw her husband on the bed. The goal was a strong, solid push. Two hands. One of our senior adults, who is seventy-five years old and has physical health issues, looked at his wife and said, "You know that wouldn't be safe for us to do. Ted is talking to younger couples. We have health considerations."

The next week another guy told me, "I appreciate your teaching last week, Pastor. My wife threw me on the bed four times and walked out of the room each time." That's not what I had in mind. However, it is refreshing to know that folks listen to the sermons from time to time.

At every marriage conference, I ask couples married for more than twenty-five years to stand. Then I work toward fifty years by saying, "If you've been married for more than thirty, remain standing. The rest of you may be seated. More than thirty-five? Forty? Forty-five? Fifty?" As we move up in years, the cheers get louder. It is fun and inspiring. The longest married couple to date at one of our events had been married for sixty-eight years. They were a precious couple from San Antonio, Texas.

I invited them to the front to win a prize. As they approached, I said, "You can choose between two books that I coauthored with Gary Smalley. Either *From Anger to Intimacy* or *The Language of Sex*." The crowd erupted with laughter and applause. Which one would they choose?

They looked at each other and giggled. They felt the pressure from the two thousand people in the crowd. The husband slowly reached up and grabbed *The Language of Sex*. The place went nuts! "I'm proud of you," I screamed out over the crowd. That sweet couple became instant rock stars! I took their picture and said, "With your permission, I'd like to post this to Facetube." The best part is they had no idea I said Facebook wrong. Everyone laughed except the couple. He nodded as if to say, "No problem." He didn't strike me as a guy carrying an iPhone.

Believe it or not, nine out of ten couples married more than fifty years grab *The Language of Sex* when asked to choose in front of a crowd. I love it! I tell Amy all the time, "I want us to hit the half-century mark, go to marriage conferences together, and choose a book on sex." About 10 percent of the time, the couple chooses *From Anger to Intimacy*. At Southeast Christian Church in February

2013 a couple married fifty-three years chose *From Anger to Intimacy*. When I joked with the husband about his choice, he snapped back at me, "Son, there ain't nothing in that book [*The Language of Sex*] I don't already know." Touché!

It would be incomplete to recognize the longest married couple and neglect the newlyweds. So I request, "If you have been married for less than twenty-five years, would you please stand?"

Once they stand, the crowd is silent. I quickly point out, "Wow, you'll notice no one applauds for you." Everyone laughs.

I continue, "If you have been married for less than twenty, remain standing. The rest of you may be seated. Less than fifteen? Ten? Five? Three? One? Six months? Last weekend? I'm just kidding." Most events, I invite a couple married a month or two to the front. All I have left to give them is *From Anger to Intimacy*. I hand it to them and say, "You won't need this until next month, but keep it handy." Everyone applauds, and the couple returns to their seats.

Messing with newlyweds brings me great joy. As they walk to the front to get their book, they hold hands and take their time. They are in love. No rush. No sense of urgency. I am quick to point that out.

"Hey, take your time; we got all night," I say. That puts a little hitch in their giddyup.

When they hit the front, I smile big and make an observation. "You two are in love, ain't ya?" They speak no words, turn to each other, and smile.

"Do you know why you two are so in love?" I ask. Before they can answer, I shout out in a loud, almost hostile voice, "Because you don't know each other." The best part is it doesn't faze them at all. The congregation laughs, and the couple skips back to their seats with a song in their hearts. Newlyweds are fun to watch and pick on.

In Song of Songs 4, Solomon and the Shulammite woman are newlyweds.

At the beginning of chapter 5 we read, "Eat, friends, and drink; drink your fill of love" (v. 1). The Hebrew word for "drink" used here means "to be intoxicated or to be saturated." It is the same word used for "satisfy" in Proverbs 5:18–19: "May your fountain be blessed, and may you rejoice in the wife of your youth. A loving doe, a graceful deer—may her breasts satisfy you always, may you ever be intoxicated with her love." God wants you to enjoy making love to your wife!

I am sick and tired of feeling as though every time we talk about sex we must go onto Satan's turf to discuss it. This ain't his turf! This is God's turf. The church has the truth on sexual intimacy. The married couples in our congregations should be known as sexually satisfied.

We have an entire chapter in our Bible that shows intoxicating sexual intimacy between a husband and wife. It instructs married couples on how to be drunk in love. In the first four verses of Song of Songs 4, we get a sneak peek into the chamber, or bedroom, of Solomon and the Shulammite woman. The scene unfolds between this newlywed couple on their honeymoon. The wife is undressing in front of her husband. Solomon shares the play-by-play.

"How beautiful you are, my darling! Oh, how beautiful! Your eyes behind your veil are doves. Your hair is like a flock of goats

descending from the hills of Gilead" (Song 4:1). The shepherd uses a word picture from his trade. In that day, Hebrew women pinned their hair up. His wife comes into the bedroom, takes the pin out, and her hair falls down around her shoulders. He pictures a flock of goats scattering down Mount Gilead. A woman's hair shares her beauty. The dropping of the hair is a seductive move. It is the first step in preparation for intimacy.

I love when Amy lets her hair down. She often asks me my opinion before her next hair appointment. I know she gets tired of the same old, same old, so I am great with her regularly changing length, style, and color. No problem here. She puts her hair up for housework, exercising, and quick trips to the store. I love that look. I also love the nighttime, when she lets it down.

Verse 2 says, *"Your teeth are like a flock of sheep just shorn, coming up from the washing. Each has its twin; not one of them is alone."* I love this. In other words, her teeth are clean, straight, and all there. That is awesome. No breath mint needed. I don't know what else you'd want from your wife's teeth than for them to be clean and straight and all there. Why does he see her teeth? She is smiling while she undresses. This once-insecure young woman is now secure as she undresses before her new husband.

She is smiling at him as she undresses. This is pretty significant because in the first chapter of the book she tells Solomon not to stare at her. *"Dark am I, yet lovely … dark like the tents of Kedar, like the tent curtains of Solomon. Do not stare at me because I am dark, because I am darkened by the sun. My mother's sons were angry with me and made me take care of the vineyards; my own vineyard [speaking of her body] I had to neglect"* (vv. 5–6).

In Solomon's day, paleness was beauty, not a suntan. They didn't go down to their local gas station and get into a tanning bed like we do here in the Ozarks. Their honeymoon is a testimony to the exclusivity in marriage. Solomon chose her. She is secure with her body in front of her husband.

Do you make love with the lights on? I think dark rooms are okay, but how much better it is to observe the facial expressions of your spouse. Since 93 percent of communication is seen in nonverbal form, it is important to see your spouse's smile, focus, or concentration prior to climax. This is where candles become your best friends. The candlelight is dim and requires squinting, but you get to visualize the body language of your spouse.

In Song of Songs 4:3, Solomon says, *"Your lips are like a scarlet ribbon; your mouth is lovely. Your temples behind your veil are like the halves of a pomegranate."* This means they are red and there is blood going through her cheeks. Verse 4 goes on to say, *"Your neck is like the tower of David, built with courses of stone; on it hang a thousand shields, all of them shields of warriors."* Solomon is speaking here of her nobility. She is not sitting down as a sheepish bride; she is looking at him with security and boldness.

Ladies, one of the best gifts you can give your husband is to undress slowly in front of him. Undressing is very sexual and a huge turn-on for guys. Don't rush. If you are insecure about your body, turn off the lights, light a votive in the far corner of the room, and make him squint.

Years ago I counseled a guy who had no idea why his wife was not turned on by him plastering himself up against the shower door. Seriously? I asked him, "Did she have a look of fright?" But now ask your husband if he would like to see you plastered up against the shower door. I bet I know his answer.

Men are turned on by confident women. I am married to a strong and confident woman. One of the false teachings of the feminist movement encourages women to find confidence deep within themselves. The problem is confidence can't be found within you. Confidence comes from the Lord, and your security is rooted in Him as the source. I am married to a sexually confident woman, and for that I am grateful.

Years ago my wife read a book called *The Sexually Confident Wife*. It is a fantastic book. As she read the book, she would ask me questions to get my input on certain issues. I'll never forget one particular night when Amy was reading the book and came upon a list of twelve different vaginal positions for couples. After reading the description of one of the positions, she started laughing and said, "I can't make out what they are talking about. Would you mind reading it and see if you can figure it out?" I grabbed the book and said, "I'd be happy to." I read through it and said, "I think, with a little stretching, we could make that work."

Women are turned on by gentleness and confidence. Verse 5 addresses the issue of gentleness: ***"Your breasts are like two fawns, like twin fawns of a gazelle that browse among the lilies."*** Why gentleness? If you want to see the fawns, you don't come running up to them, screaming and yelling. You are gentle. This is why young grooms shouldn't come out packing heat like Walker, Texas Ranger, on their honeymoon. Pastor Tommy Nelson in Denton, Texas, says, "Guys, on your honeymoon, don't come swinging out of the bathroom like Conan the Barbarian."

To be a great lover to your wife, be gentle. Men do not desire gentleness, but they do desire responsiveness. Quietness is deadly in the bedroom. He wants to know he is pleasing you, that you are enjoying it. When you have an orgasm, let him know about it. Words like "Yeah," "Oh yeah," "Oh babe," "Right there," "Perfect," and "*Yes*" signal climax. Give him verbal cues. Men learn by training. When he sees that something is pleasing you, rest assured, he will be trying that move again. He does not want to get to the end of lovemaking and go, "Oh, I'm sorry; I got there and you didn't," only to have you say you did. What!

"You did? How come you didn't let me know! I was thinking about everything from the State of the Union address to the Daytona 500, keeping my mind on something else." Men have a trick called distraction to keep them from premature ejaculation. You need to let him know.

"Until the day breaks and the shadows flee, I will go to the mountain of myrrh and to the hill of incense" (v. 6). In this verse Solomon desires intoxication by her touch and body all night long. Lovemaking is at its best when it is slow. Fast sex is okay when intentional with a quickie. However, too many quickies is like too many snacks. They are not good for the overall health and longevity of your marriage.

Again, the award for best lovemaking of the year goes to the annual getaway. Slow, unrushed, repetitive, and enduring sex is more than possible. It takes planning and concentration. The payoff is a bond that you will talk about months and even years later.

Song of Songs 4:7 shares the words every wife wants to hear from her man: ***"You are altogether beautiful, my darling; there is*** *no flaw in you.*" This is what every woman wants to hear about her body. This goes right at the insecurity a wife might have with her body image. She needs affirmation that there is no flaw in her. Once the Shulammite woman exposes her naked body to Solomon, he says, "You are perfect." Perfection has nothing to do with diets, surgeries, nips, tucks, or skin. "No flaw" is the battle cry of a man who saves his affection for one woman, his wife. He compares her to no one else. She is his! Husbanding 101 teaches me to never, ever make a disparaging remark about the body of my wife. I want the only naked body of a woman in my head to be that of Amy Cunningham. My eyes are exclusive for her alone.

Solomon builds exclusivity, security, and safety into the bedroom. Verse 8 says, *"Come with me from Lebanon, my bride, come with me from Lebanon. Descend from the crest of Amana, from the top of Senir, the summit of Hermon, from the lions' dens and the mountain haunts of leopards."* He says she will be safe with him. He is a gentle lover and allows her to create the boundaries in the bedroom.

You cannot enjoy the bedroom when fear is present. One way Amy and I keep fear out of the bedroom is by openly discussing our beliefs on sex. We both grew up pretty sheltered, and we lacked any formal discipleship or education on sex. We learned everything at school and in movies. In the FLY journal at the end of this chapter, I will give you one of the absolute best tools I know for helping couples work through the insecurities and fears in the bedroom.

Every marriage needs vigilant protection to guard against affairs. In the blink of an eye, the trust and security that are the foundation of a healthy marriage can be destroyed, and it takes years of dedicated work to rebuild that trust. There are several steps you can take to protect your marriage and bedroom.

To protect your marriage, you need to guard the marriage bed. Guys, we need to protect our wives in the bedroom and guard our hearts from sexual temptation. Make a commitment to grow closer to your wife. Be aware of your thoughts and choices every day. Draw a clear line of what you won't do, and then stay far away from it. For each person, the safety line may be a little different, but no matter who you are, you need to become accountable to someone. Everyone needs someone other than his or her spouse who can ask the difficult questions such as, "Did you compromise your standards last week?" or, "Have you been getting your emotional needs met from someone other than your mate?" Do whatever it takes to guard your marriage, your mate, and your bedroom.

"You have stolen my heart, my sister, my bride; you have stolen my heart with one glance of your eyes, with one jewel of your necklace. How delightful is your love, my sister, my bride! How much more pleasing is your love than wine, and the fragrance of your perfume more than any spice!" (vv. 9–10). Solomon continues building security. When you go back to Song of Songs 1:17, it says, *"The beams of our house are cedars; our rafters are firs,"* meaning we live in a mansion of security. He has that security in the bedroom.

The hair is let down, and the couple undresses. Now look what happens. They kiss. Kissing is a part of sexual intimacy. Song of Songs 4:11 says, *"Your lips drop sweetness as the honeycomb, my bride; milk and honey are under your tongue. The fragrance of your garments is like the fragrance of Lebanon."* The Hebrew kiss predates the French kiss by some thirteen hundred years. They enjoy a deep sensual kiss. Extended time kissing heightens foreplay, which we see in verses 12–15:

> *You are a garden locked up, my sister, my bride;*
>> *you are a spring enclosed, a sealed fountain.*
> *Your plants are an orchard of pomegranates*
>> *with choice fruits,*
>> *with henna and nard,*
>> *nard and saffron,*
>> *calamus and cinnamon,*
>> *with every kind of incense tree,*
>> *with myrrh and aloes*
>> *and all the finest spices.*
> *You are a garden fountain,*
>> *a well of flowing water*
>> *streaming down from Lebanon.*

Did you see the contrast between verse 12 and verse 15? Before marriage, you are a garden locked up. It's a great image. This is a very graphic image in verse 15. This isn't just some flowery language. He has prepared her in foreplay. She is a well of flowing water streaming down from Lebanon. Women produce a natural vaginal lubrication. We believe clearly and commentators say that's exactly what is happening here. She is prepared sexually to be with her husband. Without this natural lubrication, penetration can be painful. Again, one more reason to slow down and let this last awhile.

Here's what I love about this chapter in the Song of Songs: the reader is not present for the lovemaking. The act of intercourse is between husband, wife, and God only. *"Awake, north wind, and come, south wind!"* (v. 16). She is saying she wants him to be strong but gentle. One wind was a strong wind and the other a gentle wind.

"Blow on my garden, that its fragrance may spread everywhere" (v. 16).

They make love.

In the next chapter, with both resting side by side in bed, Solomon says, *"I have come into my garden, my sister, my bride; I have gathered my myrrh with my spice. I have eaten my honeycomb and my honey; I have drunk my wine and my milk"* (5:1).

Then God speaks. *"Eat, friends, and drink; drink your fill of love"* (5:1). He's saying, "I want you to enjoy this. I have given this to you as a gift." Great sex is the direct result of exclusivity and the security of marriage.

Amy Cunningham cannot be romanced while camping.

Women are all-day lovers. The emotional connection starts early in the morning, and nonsexual touches delivered throughout the day advance her emotions. She needs twelve nonsexual touches, and counting them disqualifies those touches. Amy likes for me to listen lovingly; help with the kids, housework, and various chores; and learn new things with her: these and many other activities prepare a woman for sex. Distractions must be removed. Domestic support needs to be provided. The bedroom must be prepared. None of that happens when we go camping.

Several years ago our family joined Amy's extended family for a camping trip to Minnesota.

We reserved a two-bedroom fishing cabin and planned to stay the week. While I enjoy spending time with family, breaking our regular routine and coordinating the schedules of twenty people are exhausting. We had a bedroom for Corynn and a bedroom for Carson. Amy and I opted to take the pullout couch in the main living area of the cabin. The entire cabin shared a one-window air-conditioning unit, which kept the inside of the cabin at eighty degrees—even at 10:00 p.m.

As we lay in bed our first night, we began romancing each other—until we discovered that we could feel every spring the bed had to offer. The full-size mattress was so uncomfortable that we decided to sleep parallel to the back of the couch. With the heat, the uncomfortable bed, and the dingy floor, I knew we weren't going to be having sex anytime soon. All we could do was laugh and be thankful that the kids were comfortable.

As far as my performance, I'd give myself a D-, but that's being generous. After driving a minivan with six people in it for eleven hours, I was too tired to prepare the room—and there wasn't much of a room to prepare. Distractions were everywhere. And did I mention that the walls were paper-thin?

But do you know what? Throughout that whole week of heat, poor sleeping conditions, and family, Amy and I flirted like crazy. We had fun with it. I never laughed more about poor performance or missed opportunities in my eleven years of marriage to her. It taught us a great lesson about freedom and flexibility. We could go the week without sex and still be great. It made me anticipate the trip home. We actually cut that vacation short by a day and a half. I was less than truthful with the family as to why we were leaving. There was no way

I was going to tell Amy's side of the family that I wanted to get home to make love to my wife.

The FLY Journal (#funlovingyou)

The Fifty-Two Sex Questions

Years ago our church decided to start teaching on marriage once a month from the pulpit. We felt it was a key strategic move to prioritize marriage in our church and homes. Now on the second Sunday of every month we stop whatever series we are in and host Twoignite Sunday.

Each Twoignite Sunday hits a topic relevant to marriage and teaches straight from Scripture. These Sundays are no-holds-barred. We get down to the nitty-gritty.

One of the best tools to come out of Twoignite is the 2Drink menu, based on Song of Songs 5:1: ***"Eat, friends, and drink; drink your fill of love."*** God wants you to be intoxicated with the body of your spouse. He wants you to enjoy sexual intimacy in marriage.

The 2Drink menu is fifty-two questions and fill-in-the-blanks for couples to start frank conversations about sex. After one Sunday morning teaching on sexual intimacy, we sent each married couple home with the menu and a two-hour burning candle. We asked them to light the candle and have a two-hour conversation about sex.

The very next Sunday, a guy from our congregation approached me and said, "Hey, Ted, I found out that if you light that candle under a ceiling fan, the conversation only takes about forty-five minutes." I love the creativity of our members.

Since that Sunday, this menu is now the most requested resource and download on our website. Even though the menu was designed to ignite conversation, we are regularly asked to give our answers to the questions. This is good and bad. On one hand, some of these questions do not have right or wrong answers. On the other hand, people want to know what's "normal." I understand. Couples need to talk to each other and consult Scripture to figure out what's normal for them.

I recommend that you read through all fifty-two questions individually first. Circle any question that you consider off-limits. When you come together to discuss, respect each other's boundaries with the circled items.

Appetizers (Safe Questions)

1. Is sex an embarrassing subject for you?
2. How often, if ever, did you and your parents talk about sex?
3. What kind of picture did your parents paint for you about sex?
4. When and where did you first learn about sex?
5. Are there any questions about sex that you think are off-limits for us to discuss?
6. Give an example of an off-limits question.
7. What parts of your body are you insecure about? What can I do to ease those insecurities?
8. Do you like it when I undress in front of you? Should I slow it down?

9. Do you like what I wear leading up to sex? (Should I burn the sweats?)

10. What would you change about our bedroom to spice it up?

Frequency

The best question we are asked on our website is, "How often should an evangelical couple have sex?" Great question. Compared to other world religions, I have no idea. But I do believe that Christian couples need to prioritize sexual intimacy and make love more often.

11. On a scale of 1 to 10, how satisfied are you with how often we have sex?

12. I enjoy having sex ____ times per week or month.

13. How often do you reach climax when we make love?

14. Have you ever been frustrated thinking tonight's the night only to be disappointed? Does this happen often?

15. What time of day is the best time for you?

16. What should our code phrases be around the kids on the night we are in the mood? (For example, "Let's work on the budget tonight," or, "Do we need anything at the supermarket?" Nobody uses the word *supermarket* anymore, so that works.)

17. Do we do well sharing the initiation?

18. Do we offer grace to each other when "tonight's the night" doesn't work out? Do we ever show anger?

Performance

19. On a scale of 1 to 10, how satisfied are you with our performance?

20. What can we do to bring our sex life out of a rut?

21. Can you give me two or three ideas for foreplay?

22. Do I move through foreplay too quickly? Or is it too much time?

23. What gets you in the mood more than anything?

24. What are some practical ways we can prepare the bedroom for lovemaking?

25. What position is most comfortable for you?

26. Do you prefer to be on top or on bottom?

27. Should we sleep nude more often?

28. Should we shower together?

29. Am I too rough when I kiss or massage your breasts?

30. Is there anything I ever do that makes you uncomfortable or causes you pain?

31. What sounds do you like hearing to know that I am enjoying it?

32. Should we use more candles?

33. What genre of music would you want on our lovemaking playlist?

34. Lotions, oils, scents? You in?

35. I like it best when you _____ (after a few years the list is five pages long).

36. It makes me uncomfortable when you _____.

37. What are the distractions that keep us from getting together?

38. Are you interested in me rubbing or lightly massaging your clitoris?

39. Are you okay with sex outside?

40. Is oral sex okay with you?

41. What can we do to be more creative?

42. Who sets the boundaries for creativity?

Endurance

43. On a scale of 1 to 10, how satisfied are you with how long we spend making love?

44. Do you ever feel like we rush it?

45. On the days when life is crazy and when it has been a while since we have been intimate, are you good with quickies?

46. What concerns do you have about quickies?

47. How long should sex last?

48. Have you ever been frustrated at how long it takes me to get in the mood?

49. Have you ever been frustrated at how long it takes me to reach climax?

50. What are some other techniques we need to add to our foreplay?

51. How can I gain ejaculatory control?

52. Is getting there at the same time important?

Chapter 9

A Marriage and Funeral Worth Repeating

A good name is better than fine perfume, and the
day of death better than the day of birth.

—Ecclesiastes 7:1

So far, we've been really doing the hard work of figuring out how to have fun in marriage. To sum up:

Enjoying an evening out with your spouse is fun.

Sharing a meal paired with wine is fun.

Getting away for a weekend to make love is fun.

Laughing at a joke with your spouse is fun.

Most couples have fun moments as part of their marriage story. Most couples have fun seasons as part of their marriage story. The goal of this book is to learn how to enjoy each other for a lifetime. That is why we end our time together with a funeral.

Amy and I are grateful for parents and grandparents who honor, enjoy, and prioritize marriage. We are blessed to say that Dennis and Linda Freitag, Ron and Bonnie Cunningham, Roland and Erliss Kelzenberg, William and Millie Cunningham, Earl and Mary Jane Ludwig, and Lloyd and Lorraine Freitag honored their vows for life. That is rare nowadays. I don't say that to bash your family history, not at all! I say that to remind you that enjoying marriage for a lifetime is more than possible.

I dedicated this book to Lloyd and Lorraine Freitag, a couple who enjoyed life together for over sixty-five years.

Lloyd was a fun, loving guy. Towering over six feet tall, he had a gentle spirit that warmed the hardest of hearts. He had a signature wink. Not a subtle wink, but a lean-forward, tilt-the-head, lift-the-corner-of-his-mouth-type wink. He gave it to everyone. His wife, children, grandchildren, and great-grandchildren knew a wink from Grandpa Lloyd meant, "I love and appreciate you."

I call it the "honor wink." At times it was flirtatious with his wife. At other times it spoke blessing. It was also a simple thank-you for a store clerk or to someone holding open a door. Whatever the case, it was a wink that said, "You are valuable!"

Lloyd learned honor and respect as a kid and during his time in the navy during the latter part of World War II. He answered the call like countless men and women who put life on hold to save the world for us. He never complained about his service. It was his honor to defend our country and fight for freedom. Countless times in Branson, Missouri, I witnessed Lloyd standing at the request of an entertainer wishing to honor the vets. He was proud of his service.

He came home from the war and took a job at Hormel Foods in Austin, Minnesota, where he worked for forty-one years and seven months. Lloyd learned his hard-work ethic from his dad, Elmer, who worked in the same Hormel plant for forty-seven years. Lloyd was there the day his dad retired. It was an emotional day because Elmer didn't want to go, but they forced him to take early retirement. That still cracks me up that he considered being forced out after forty-seven years "early retirement." That generation sure knew how to work hard.

More astounding than Lloyd's service to his country and his work at Hormel was his commitment to a redhead named Lorraine. They absolutely loved and enjoyed each other.

They went on their first date on a Saturday night in September 1946. They dated for an entire week when Lloyd asked, "Are we going to get serious about this relationship or what?"

"What do you mean?" Lorraine asked.

"Do you want to get married?" He popped the question just like that.

She said, "Yes."

The rest is history.

In September 2011, Lloyd and Lorraine celebrated sixty-five years of marriage. It takes a real man to love and enjoy the same woman for sixty-five years. What a fantastic testimony to his children, grandchildren, and great-grandchildren.

We celebrated his eighty-seventh birthday that same year with cake and ice cream at a rehabilitation care facility just two blocks from his home. In typical Lloyd fashion, when we sang him the birthday song, he joined right in. When we got to the "Happy birthday, dear

Lloyd" part, he sang "Happy birthday, dear me." I have the video on my iPhone to prove it.

We almost lost him on his birthday. The physical therapist made him work out on a stationary bike with an empty oxygen tank.

Hello?

When we arrived at his room, he told me, "They dang near killed me." He was smiling because he found great humor in the mishap. Imagine surviving the Great Depression and World War II only to be taken out by a first-year physical therapist forgetting to fill your oxygen tank. Only Lloyd could find the humor in that.

I remember leaving the care facility that day. Amy and I were both a little teary eyed. As we walked out of his room and down the hall a few steps, we heard him say, "I sure do love you kids."

On June 13, 2012, we received a call from Austin, Minnesota. The doctors were giving Lloyd only a day or two to live. For two years he had suffered from congestive heart failure, and this was the end. We expected this call.

We immediately packed up the car in Branson and drove our family, including Amy's parents, to the Mayo Clinic in Rochester, Minnesota. It was a sobering ten-hour drive knowing that we were going to say good-bye to Grandpa Lloyd. We told Lloyd-stories the whole way there. We laughed and cried. I had lost three of my grandparents; this was to be Amy's first.

Early on the morning of June 14, we all walked into room 738 to say good morning and good-bye to Grandpa. Denny, my wife's dad, was the first to hug and kiss his dad. Then Amy and the kids took their turn to say, "I love you."

As I approached the bed and placed my hand on Lloyd's, he said, "Ted, is there any way you can speed this up?" Even on his deathbed, Lloyd continued to have a great sense of humor.

We spent most of the day gathered around Grandpa, telling stories and giving an overdose of meaningful touch. After dinner that night, I dropped off Denny at the hospital so he and his dad could watch the Minnesota Twins game together. Father and son holding hands for one last ball game. I picture that scene in my mind but sixty years earlier. How many times did Lloyd hold little Denny's hand on the way into a game? As Denny sat there that night, he knew that the days go slow, but the years go so fast.

The next morning we got up early and headed back to the hospital. Lloyd asked that this be the day they stopped trying so hard to keep him alive. The doctors met and agreed to honor Lloyd's request.

With his wife, children, grandchildren, and great-grandchildren circled around the bed, we prayed, took the Lord's Supper, sang, and received a blessing from Grandpa.

After our family worship service, Lloyd took out his oxygen tubes and hearing aids and said, "Good-bye, everyone, I gotta go." Three hours later he saw Jesus face-to-face.

I have been a pastor for seventeen years now, and I can say without a doubt that Lloyd's death was the best death I have ever been a part of in my ministry and life. Many families do not receive this sort of time and opportunity to say good-bye. I get that. We were double blessed by Lloyd. A lot families wait for this love and affection at the deathbed. With Lloyd, this was his life. Our grateful and loving good-bye was simply one more validation to a life well lived.

I will never forget Lloyd kissing his wife and blessing his children. I know I don't get to choose how I go out, but, boy, oh boy, I would like to go out like that.

Tears flowed as our family's season of mourning began. We were a mess. When we stepped into the hall, my eight-year-old daughter, Corynn, asked her seven-year-old brother, Carson, "Why are you the only one not crying?"

"Sissy, I have learned to control my emotions," he said with confidence.

This was the first time my children witnessed death. Corynn has the mercy gift. For most of the day she stood by Grandpa's bedside and rested her hand on his while stroking his arm. On the wall in front of the bed hung cards and notes that read, "I love you." Lloyd could not escape the love of his family. Why? Because he was a loving and fun grandpa who lived a life of duty, loyalty, sacrifice, commitment, and honor. Giving it back to him was an overflow of what he gave us.

On the day of his death, the family asked that I preach at Lloyd's funeral. What an honor! One I did not take lightly. I knew it would be hard to hold it together, but the content would be easy. A life well lived means a life well celebrated. I've officiated tough funerals of men and women who did not know the Lord. I've officiated funerals of men and women who were estranged from their families. It is not easy to get up and speak to a nearly empty funeral home about a man you didn't know and in turn didn't know Jesus. That would not be the case with Lloyd.

The funeral was the following week at St. Olaf Lutheran Church in Austin, Minnesota. Here I was, a young punk preacher with shirt untucked, smack-dab in the middle of a liturgical funeral at a historic church. The weight of this day was upon me.

The pastor asked that I start with a Scripture reading, then go into my message. I started with the same passage I read at every funeral, Ecclesiastes 7:1–4:

> A good name is better than fine perfume,
>> and the day of death better than the day of
>> birth.
> It is better to go to a house of mourning
>> than to go to a house of feasting,
> for death is the destiny of everyone;
>> the living should take this to heart.
> Frustration is better than laughter,
>> because a sad face is good for the heart.
> The heart of the wise is in the house of mourning,
>> but the heart of fools is in the house of
>> pleasure.

What does it mean to take death to heart? Why is a funeral better than a party? Simple. You learn great life lessons at a funeral. No one ever walks out of a comedy club or party and says, "That changed my life." That is not the purpose of laughter or cutting up with friends. Proverbs calls that levity "good medicine" (17:22). But when you go to a funeral, you ask questions about your own life. Am I living well? Will anyone say nice things about me when I'm gone? Will I have this many people at my funeral? Did I say everything to Grandpa I should have said? Did he know how much I loved him?

Funerals recalibrate life's priorities. The frantic pace of life changes and everything goes on hold when we get the call that a loved one died. Chasing a buck seems senseless. Squabbling over finances is a waste of time. Lloyd's life and death brought us perspective.

Lloyd never wrote a book. He did not travel the country speaking as an expert on any particular subject. He never ran for office, competed in professional sports, or recorded a best-selling album. Nonetheless, Lloyd was my hero. He was the patriarch of our family, and he got it right. He enjoyed life with his wife, led his family, and loved his neighbors and friends.

As the funeral continued, I encouraged Lorraine with the words of Solomon: "Enjoy life with your wife, whom you love, all the days of this meaningless life" (Eccles. 9:9). Lloyd was more than committed to Lorraine. Sure they spent sixty-five years together, but more than that he loved and enjoyed her. On the day of his death he kissed her multiple times and gave her his signature wink.

Lloyd hunted, fished, trapped, camped, metal detected, and rode Harleys. He and Lorraine toured the country together on a Harley for years. They were companions in everything.

We have much to learn from Lloyd. He was a gracious, kind, and loving man. He enjoyed life and his family. As I was preparing for the funeral, my wife reminded me of something Jesus said: "You will be known as My disciples by the way you love one another" (John 13:35, author's translation). Of all the preachers I know and after growing up in the church, I can honestly say that Lloyd modeled the love of Jesus Christ more than any man or woman I have ever known.

I love that moment in a funeral when sorrow briefly turns to joy. It's not that our mourning is over, but we have a glimpse of joy in knowing Lloyd is with Jesus and we will see him again one day. I ended the preaching portion of the funeral with 1 Thessalonians 4:13–18:

> Brothers and sisters, we do not want you to be uninformed about those who sleep in death, so that you do not grieve like the rest of mankind, who have no hope. For we believe that Jesus died and rose again, and so we believe that God will bring with Jesus those who have fallen asleep in him. According to the Lord's word, we tell you that we who are still alive, who are left until the coming of the Lord, will certainly not precede those who have fallen asleep. For the Lord himself will come down from heaven, with a loud command, with the voice of the archangel and with the trumpet call of God, and the dead in Christ will rise first. After that, we who are still alive and are left will be caught up together with them in the clouds to meet the Lord in the air. And so we will be with the Lord forever. Therefore encourage one another with these words.

We grieved with hope at Lloyd's funeral. Our hope is in the fact that Jesus died and rose again. With that we celebrate a life well lived.

Lloyd had two children, Denny and Deanna. He had four grandchildren, Jenny, Brian, Amy (my wife), and Ginia. He had eight great-grandchildren, Haley, Dakota, Connor, Corynn, Carson,

Avery, Jada, and Bria. My sermon ended with a personal address to the children, grandchildren, and great-grandchildren: "How do we take to heart the death of Grandpa Freitag? We place our faith in Jesus, return home, work hard, enjoy our spouses, and love and bless our children." After that we sang "How Great Thou Art" and headed to our cars lined up in front of the church.

As we arrived graveside, there stood nine guys from the VFW (Veterans of Foreign Wars). Seven held guns for the gun salute, one held a folded flag, and the other a bugle. The honor guard is part of many funerals I officiate, but I still choke back tears when a frail veteran presents a pristine folded flag to the widow and says, "On behalf of the president of the United States and the chief of Naval Operations, please accept this flag as a symbol of our appreciation for your loved one's service to this country and a grateful navy."

When it was all said and done, Amy's uncle Wayne approached me and asked, "Hey, Ted, make me a promise. Will you do my funeral that well?"

I quickly responded with, "You've got some work to do."

We smiled and laughed because we knew we both had much to live up to. Lloyd demonstrated a life with Lorraine that we admired. We wanted our lives and marriages to reflect the same. Thank you, Lloyd and Lorraine, for a life and marriage well lived!

It sounds strange to end a fun book on marriage with a funeral. Trust me, I've wrestled with the best way to share this story. This chapter has the most prayer poured into it. I asked the Lord to give me the words to encourage you to go the distance in your marriage. Not just to divorce-proof your home, but to enjoy your marriage for a lifetime.

The FLY Journal (#funlovingyou)

Do we have parents or grandparents who lived life well?

Name a few couples we know who honor, prioritize, and enjoy marriage.

In a few words, how would our children describe our marriage?

Do we have a marriage that our children would say is worth repeating?

If not, what steps are we taking toward a fun, loving marriage?

Notes

Chapter 1: Love, Laughter, and a Trampoline

1. Norman Cousins, *Anatomy of an Illness as Perceived by the Patient: Reflections on Healing and Regeneration* (New York: W. W. Norton, 1979), 43–44. Quoted by Drs. Les and Leslie Parrott in *The Love List* (Colorado Springs: Focus on the Family, 2002).

2. Charles Swindoll, *Day by Day* (Nashville: Thomas Nelson, 2000), 339.

3. Charles Swindoll, as quoted in Martin H. Manser, comp., *The Westminster Collection of Christian Quotations: Over 6000 Quotations Arranged by Theme* (Louisville, KY: Westminster John Knox, 2001), 225.

4. Agnes Repplier , as quoted by Drs. Les and Leslie Parrott in *The Love List* (Colorado Springs: Focus on the Family, 2002).

Chapter 2: The Unstuck Marriage

1. Stoyan Zaimov, "Pope Benedict XVI Turns 85, Admits He's on 'Final Leg' of Life," CP Europe, accessed May 10, 2013, http://global.christianpost.com/news/pope-benedict-xvi-turns-85-admits-hes-on-final-leg-of-life-73357/#Y1FOgvsIXs4YT2Py.99.

Chapter 3: The Fun Loving You Lists

1. "The 40 Biggest Duets of All Time," Billboard, accessed May 13, 2013, www.billboard.com/articles/list/473075/the-40-biggest-duets-of-all-time.

Chapter 4: The Daily Getaway

1. "Song of Songs," in the NET Bible, Bible.org, accessed May 12, 2013, http://bible.org/download/netbible/ondemand/bybook/sos.pdf, 1231.

Chapter 5: The Weekly Getaway (Date Night Challenge)

1. W. Bradford Wilcox and Jeffrey Dew, "The Date Night Opportunity: What Does Couple Time Tell Us about the Potential Value of Date Nights?," University of Virginia, accessed May 12, 2013, http://nationalmarriageproject.org/wp-content/uploads/2012/05/NMP-DateNight.pdf, 3.

2. Wilcox and Dew, "Date Night," 4.

3. Wilcox and Dew, "Date Night," 4.

4. Wilcox and Dew, "Date Night," 4.

5. Wilcox and Dew, "Date Night," 5.

6. "The 40 Biggest Duets of All Time," Billboard, accessed May 13, 2013, www.billboard.com/articles/list/473075/the-40-biggest-duets-of-all-time.

Chapter 6: The Annual Getaway

1. Nancy Trejos, "Travel Can Improve Couples' Sex Life, Survey Says," *USA Today*, accessed May 14, 2013, www.usatoday.com/story/travel/2013/02/07/valentines-day-travel/1893591.

2. Davyd Foard Hood, "National Historic Landmark Nomination of the Biltmore Estate," National Park Service, www.nps.gov/history/nhl/designations/samples/nc/Biltmore.pdf.

Scripture Index

Chapter 8: The Fun (and Safe) Bedroom

Chapter 9: A Marriage and Funeral Worth Repeating

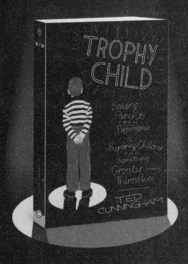